COVER-UP:

The Politics of
Pearl Harbor,
1941-1946

COVER-UP:

The Politics of
Pearl Harbor,
1941-1946

Bruce R. Bartlett

ARLINGTON HOUSE·PUBLISHERS
NEW ROCHELLE, NEW YORK

Book design by Pat Slesarchik

Manufactured in the United States of America
P 10 9 8 7 6 5 4 3 2 1

Library of Congress Cataloging in Publication Data

Bartlett, Bruce R., 1951-
  Cover-up.

  Bibliography: p.
  Includes index.
  1. Pearl Harbor, Attack on, 1941. 2. United
States—Politics and government—1933–1953.
3. Roosevelt, Franklin Delano, Pres. U. S., 1882–
1945. I. Title.
D767.92.B343   940.54'26   78–23677
ISBN 0–87000–423–9

Contents

Foreword

In 1944 I moved to Washington with a free-roving assignment to do text pieces for *Life* magazine. Since I had differed in a publicly circulated memo with Harry Luce over the implications of his famous interventionist essay on "The American Century," my luck in getting such a choice berth was the subject of some eyebrow-raising comment in the New York offices of Mr. Luce's publications. But Harry Luce's loyalty, as an editor, was always to the story—he was the least personal editor I have ever known. He was very much like Franklin D. Roosevelt in his liking to keep representatives of all points of view on tap: thus he maintained Teddy White on his payroll—and printed his articles—long after he and Teddy had come to disagree about Chiang Kai-shek's China. If he could continue to use Teddy he could still use me.

It was with some diffidence, nonetheless, that I sent a memo to Harry Luce in late 1944 about some gossip I had picked up about Pearl Harbor. I thought I had a scoop in hand, but doubted that Luce would like it for what I considered its isolationist implications. Isaac Don Levine, the man who touched off the Hiss case by persuading Whittaker Chambers to tell his story of Soviet penetration of the State Department to Adolf Berle, had held a party for his wife Ruth and myself, who happen to share the same birthday. One of Don's Army friends at the party was in a loquacious mood. Apparently thinking he was talking off the record, this friend, a colonel, went into some detail about the great "secret" the Republicans had failed to exploit. Briefly, the Republican candidate for president, New York Gov. Tom Dewey, had known that the White House had been forewarned of the 1941 Japanese attack in time to save our Pacific Fleet from destruction if only the word had been given to our commanders in Hawaii. But Dewey had patriotically refrained from making political use of his knowledge because of his uncertainty about the impact on our code-cracking in the Pacific. We had broken the Japanese "ultra" code in 1941, and neither Dewey nor his political manager Herbert Brownell was in a position to know whether the Japanese were still using "ultra" in 1944.

Knowing nothing at the time about the nine lives of the modern code machine, I felt it most unlikely that the Japanese had gone on using the same old signals in the course of a long war. If our code-cracking handiwork was not actually at stake, Dewey had palpably been hornswoggled out of a campaign issue. I thought Luce might see it that way. But he reacted as Dewey himself had reacted. He told me to keep my information quiet until after the war.

Right after the Japanese surrender, the following August, Luce was on the phone to me. He told me to pick Tom Dewey up at the Elmira Reformatory, where he was on a tour of inspection. After an all-night ride on an uncomfortable Erie coach I caught up with Dewey in time to ride with him along Lake Seneca. In an hour I had been told of the visits of Col. Carter Clarke, General Marshall's emissary, who had brought the letters that persuaded Dewey to keep the Pearl Harbor issue out of the 1944 presidential campaign. Dewey said I could use the story, but on a nonattribution basis.

So *Life* printed a long account of the first phases of what Bruce Bartlett calls a "cover-up." Aside from John T. Flynn's pamphlets on the subject, which the *Chicago Tribune* syndicated, the *Life* story provided the first detailed information about something the Roosevelt Administration had managed to keep quiet through four years of war.

There was a justification for a cover-up as long as the war was on, even though the administration acted heartlessly in trying to make scapegoats of Admiral Kimmel and General Short, the two commanders in Hawaii who had no knowledge of our code-breaking feat. But what about the conduct of the big postwar congressional investigation of Pearl Harbor, which had Sen. Homer Ferguson, the Michigan Republican, scratching for evidence that Franklin Roosevelt was busy all through 1941 trying to get us into the war with Nazi Germany by backdoor pressure on the Japanese in the Pacific? I covered the investigation in order to do a *Life* article about Senator Ferguson called "The Man Who Pushed Pearl Harbor." There was never any proof that Roosevelt had set up our Pacific Fleet for the attack. The evidence seemed to be that the war would break in the Philippines or in the East Indies. But Ferguson came close to paydirt when he brought Comdr. Lester Schulz, who had been the naval aide on duty at the White House on the night of December 6, 1941, back from his ship, the *Indiana,* to testify that he had personally delivered a final Japanese intercept to Roosevelt and Harry Hopkins. Schulz recalled that Roosevelt had read the message and remarked to Hopkins, in substance, that "this means war." When Hopkins suggested that Washington could surprise the Japanese by striking the first blow, Roosevelt said, in effect, "No, we can't do that. We are a democracy and a peaceful people. But we have a good record." In other words, we could best serve a larger purpose by taking it on the chin.

It was obvious to Homer Ferguson that Roosevelt wanted a Pacific issue that would justify going to the rescue of Churchill in the Atlantic. An effort to get Adm. Tommy Hart, our naval commander in the Far East, to deploy three useless reconnaissance ships as decoys to invite an overt act from some trigger-happy Japanese aviator was a revealing Roosevelt move.

Ironically, if Ferguson had only looked elsewhere, to the Atlantic, he would have found plenty of evidence that Franklin Roosevelt had acted unneutrally—and quite illegally—to align us in the war against the Axis powers without a declaration from Congress. The story of how Roosevelt put an American plane, a Catalina with an American commander, at the service of the British Admiralty in tracking down the Nazi warship *Bismarck* is a flagrant example. And there are others in two recent books, *A Man Called Intrepid* by William Stevenson, and *Bodyguard of Lies* by Anthony Cave Brown. Ferguson was not wrong in his suspicions. He was merely one ocean away from his true quarry.

So the story of Pearl Harbor is part of a larger Roosevelt cover-up. Whether FDR was wiser than the rest of us in trying to force a war against Hitler and the Japanese is a good question. But there is no doubt that he did act undemocratically, both in the Atlantic and the Pacific. He knew what he was doing, and he admitted as much to Robert Sherwood when he wondered audibly if he would be impeached because of his action in aiding the *Bismarck* hunt. His justification for his actions was precisely on a par with Nixon's in the Watergate cover-up: State concern for the public safety imposed on a commander-in-chief.

Harry Luce had no intention of letting me use a Pearl Harbor *Life* article to make a case for continued isolationism. He felt, quite rightly as I came to see it, that what Pearl Harbor called for was a far more honest integration of foreign and military policy and popular understanding. We didn't have this in 1941, when FDR was hiding things from the people and there was no CIA to assess the significance of the red flag that Navy Comdr. Alwin Kramer, who translated Japanese intercepts, placed on a so-called bomb-plot message that divided Pearl Harbor into subareas, presumably to guide incoming bombers.

Bruce Bartlett's book does a masterly job in delineating what various groups hoped to gain from a Pearl Harbor inquiry. The isolationists were set on resuming the suspended arguments of 1941. The Republicans hoped to use the inquiry to throw Democrats out of office. The Democrats, fighting back, were intent on protecting the memory of FDR.

Neither the isolationists nor the FDR partisans got what they wanted. The reason is that the victors of World War II are still quarreling over the spoils. The war is far from being over, and the intercontinental ballistic missile could be the final arbiter in the quarrel of the victors. It is not the same world as in 1941, when physical isolation of the North American continent was a possibility. As for Roosevelt's reputation, it will depend on what happens to the present democratic-totalitarian confrontation. If we fought one dictator only to succumb to another, it will call for some real revisionism. The revision, of course, would have to be done by a *samizdat* author in some Gulag camp, and it would be of great help if he could have a smuggled copy of Bruce Bartlett's book at his elbow.

JOHN CHAMBERLAIN

Acknowledgments

The present book began as an undergraduate thesis while I was a senior at Rutgers University. Reading Harry Elmer Barnes' *Perpetual War for Perpetual Peace* and Charles Beard's *President Roosevelt and the Coming of the War, 1941,* had motivated me to investigate the origins of World War II. A short time later I discovered that Percy L. Greaves, who had written a chapter for the Barnes book and headed the minority staff of the Joint Committee on the Investigation of the Pearl Harbor Attack, lived close by. I came to know Greaves, and he was of great assistance to me in my study of the complexities of the Pearl Harbor issue (to which this book is only an introduction).

At that time I was fortunate also to be associated with several very fine professors who were sympathetic to my efforts, if not necessarily in agreement with my views. I learned much from Professors Warren Kimball, Lloyd Gardner, Richard Stone and Richard Kohn, and owe them much gratitude.

My work on Pearl Harbor continued while I was a graduate student at Georgetown University. I'm sure my decision to attend that particular university was somewhat influenced by the fact that it was there that Prof. Charles C. Tansill, author of *Back Door to War,* had taught until his death. The core of this book (chapters four through seven) is derived from my Master's thesis, which was completed in May 1976. Once again I was fortunate in having professors sympathetic to my efforts. In particular, I am grateful to Prof. Jules Davids for acting as my advisor on this project.

Along the way I have received valuable financial support from the Institute for Humane Studies, Menlo Park, California, and the Liberty Fund, Indianapolis, Indiana. Most of the research and

11

writing for this book was done while I was a Liberty Fund Fellow at the Institute for Humane Studies in 1975. This fellowship was especially important in giving me the opportunity to do some archival research that otherwise I could not have attempted. I wish to sincerely thank Ken Templeton of the institute for his help and encouragement.

I would like to be able to acknowledge here all of those who gave me aid and encouragement, but since the number is large, I can only mention a few by name: Capt. Thomas K. Kimmel, USN (ret.), Judge Gerhard Gesell, Judge Homer Ferguson, Thomas D. Flynn, Justus Doenecke, Robert D. Stuart, Leonard Liggio, Edward Hanify, Willard Edwards, John E. Masten, Edward P. Morgan, Charles C. Hiles, Adm. Kemp Tolley, USN (ret.), Richard Whalen, Forrest Pogue, Adolph Hoeling and William Marina.

Special thanks go to Karl Pflock, my highly competent editor at Arlington House; Sharon Zelaska, who typed the manuscript; and John Chamberlain, for his gracious foreword.

I

Pre-Pearl Harbor Politics

The 1930s are usually thought of as a period of isolationism. Unfortunately, this tells us very little about what was really happening during that decade. Yet the very characterization of the debate as between "isolationism" and "internationalism" is not without significance, for the words themselves have positive and negative connotations quite apart from the issues involved. They are, in fact, code words designed to evoke a response, in the same way that Pavlov's dogs reacted to the ringing of a bell. As Lloyd Gardner has written, "Labels such as 'isolationism,' 'interventionism,' and 'internationalism' have been supplied to give us substitutes for careful analysis."[1]

The truth is that twentieth century isolationism was not a carefully thought out philosophy, although its philosophical roots can be traced back at least to George Washington's Farewell Address.[2] Rather, it was a reaction to events and circumstances. In particular, it was a reaction to the First World War.

The First World War was perhaps the greatest watershed in American history. It marked the beginning of America's large-scale influence in world affairs, the unleashing of great forces (such as communism) that continue to exert major influence on the world, and the origin of the leviathan state, with all of the governmental interference in our personal and economic relations that go with it.

The reaction against this situation was neither illogical, irrational, nor foolish. Those who opposed American entry into World War II understood very clearly the importance of the changes that had been wrought on American life by our involvement in World War I, and they rightly feared the consequences of another major conflict. In an extremely perceptive analysis by someone who could hardly be called an isolationist, George F. Kennan has said as much. In discussing the impact of the two world wars he wrote:

> These wars were fought at the price of some tens of millions of lives, of untold physical destruction, of the destruction of the balance of forces on the Continent—at the price of rendering western Europe dangerously, perhaps fatefully, vulnerable to Soviet power. Both wars were fought, really, with a view to changing Germany: to correcting her behavior, to making the Germans something different from what they were. Yet, today, if one were offered the chance of having back again the Germany of 1913—a Germany run by conservative but relatively moderate people, no Nazis and no Communists, a vigorous Germany, united and unoccupied, full of energy and confidence, able to play a part again in the balancing-off of Russian power in Europe—well, there would be objections to it from many quarters, and it wouldn't make everybody happy; but in many ways it wouldn't sound so bad, in comparison with our problems of today. Now, think what this means. When you tally up the total score of the two wars, in terms of their ostensible objective, you find that if there has been any gain at all, it is pretty hard to discern.
>
> Does this not mean that something is terribly wrong here? Can it really be that all this bloodshed and sacrifice was just the price of sheer survival for the Western democracies in the twentieth century? If we were to accept that conclusion, things would look pretty black; for we would have to ask ourselves: Where does all this end? If this was the price of surival in the first half of the twentieth century, what is survival going to cost us in the second half? But plainly this immense output of effort and sacrifice should have brought us something more than just survival. And then, we can only assume, some great miscalculations must have been made somewhere? But where? Were they ours? Were they our Allies'?[3]

Disillusionment

Although disillusionment with World War I began shortly after the conflict ended, with the refusal of the United States Senate to ratify the Versailles Treaty and to permit the U.S. to join the

League of Nations, the public at large did not really begin to apprehend the futility of the "war to end all wars" until the 1930s. Under the influence of revisionist writers like Walter Millis, who wrote the bestselling *Road to War,* and Sen. Gerald P. Nye's sensational investigation of the role of the munitions industry in bringing the U.S. into the war, the public generally adopted a position of neutrality toward any future war that did not involve an actual attack on American territory. No longer would the United States become involved in European wars.

This position remained fairly consistent right down to Pearl Harbor eve. For example, in a national poll taken in February 1937, people were asked: "If another war like the World War develops in Europe, should America take part again?" An overwhelming 95 percent of the people said no. In April 1939 they were asked: "If England and France should go to war against Germany, do you think this country should declare war on Germany?" Again, 95 percent said no. A year later, in June 1940, after war had been raging in Europe for more than eight months, people were asked: "If the question of the United States going to war against Germany and Italy came up for a national vote within the next two or three weeks, would you vote to go into the war or to stay out of the war?" Eight-six percent of those questioned said no. And as late as August 1941, when asked: "If you were asked to vote today on the question of the United States entering the war now against Germany and Italy, how would you vote—to go to war now, or stay out?" 75 percent of the people wanted to stay out. Seventy-six percent responded negatively when asked about war with Japan.[4]

The Neutrality Acts

Catering to this sentiment, the Congress passed neutrality acts designed to make sure America stayed out of war. These acts were designed to prevent a recurrence of the situation that had arisen in 1917 in which—it was believed—private interests in the United States had such a great vested interest in the outcome of the war, because of loans and other financial arrangements, that they strongly influenced the U.S. government to enter the war on the side of Britain and France. As the report of the Nye Committee concluded:

Loans to belligerents mitigate against neutrality, for when only one group of belligerents can purchase and transport commodities, the loans act in favor of that belligerent. They are especially unneutral when used to convert this country into an auxiliary arsenal for that belligerent who happens to control the seas, for that arsenal then becomes the subject of the military strategy of the other belligerent.[5]

The first Neutrality Act was passed in 1935. This act required the president to proclaim, at the outbreak of hostilities between two or more foreign countries, an embargo of arms and munitions to all belligerents, and a prohibition on the export of such material in American ships. Furthermore, at his option he could extend this embargo to other countries entering the war, close American ports to foreign submarines, and warn American citizens against traveling in the ships of belligerents.[6]

The Neutrality Act was extended and reinforced in February 1936 and May 1937. The 1937 act continued the embargo on export of arms and munitions and extended a "cash-and-carry" principle to all other goods. Thenceforth, belligerent nations had to pay cash for whatever goods they bought in the United States and transport them in their own ships. It was believed that this measure would safeguard for all time American neutrality in a foreign conflict and prevent the United States from being drawn into any war by economic interests.[7]

While probably disapproving of the Neutrality Acts through 1937, there is no evidence that President Franklin D. Roosevelt disagreed with their general purpose.[8] In October of that year, however, he made a change of course by suggesting greater involvement by the United States in the growing world crisis. This was the famous speech in Chicago in which Roosevelt openly called for the "quarantine" of aggressor nations.[9] But the reaction of the American people to this intimation of American involvement was swift and negative, further evidencing the anti-interventionist mood of the people.[10] And the extent to which it caused the president to back off from any further excursions into interventionism may be shown by his unwillingness to raise the issue of intervention throughout the rest of 1937—even through the *Panay* incident, in which an American gunboat was sunk by the Japanese.[11]

The Drift Toward Intervention

Throughout 1938 and 1939 Roosevelt tried to enunciate a more interventionist policy, but he was forced to move slowly lest he incur the wrath of the people. Nevertheless, slow but steady progress was made toward greater American involvement. In 1939 Roosevelt succeeded in getting a revision of the Neutrality Act that lifted the absolute embargo on munitions sales to belligerent nations.[12] By 1940 he was committed to helping the Allies at all costs. The necessity of getting reelected, however, caused his rhetoric to be a good bit more anti-interventionist than his actions.

This contrast was especially evident during the fall of 1940. On September 3 Roosevelt announced the destroyers-for-bases deal—which involved trading fifty overage American destroyers in return for leases on several British bases in the Western Hemisphere—clearly an interventionist act. Then, on October 30, he reassured a Boston audience about his desire to maintain American neutrality:

> And while I am talking to you mothers and fathers, I will give you one more assurance.
> I have said this before, but I shall say it again and again and again: Your boys are not going to be sent into any foreign wars.[13]

As a consequence of this wide divergence between Roosevelt's words and actions, some of his own supporters became concerned. His speechwriter, the well-known playwright Robert Sherwood, later said: "Perhaps he might have done a better and more candid job of presenting his case. For my own part, I think it was a mistake for him to go so far in yielding to the hysterical demands for sweeping reassurance; but, unfortunately for my own conscience, I happened at the time to be one of those who urged him to go the limit on this, feeling as I did that any risk of future embarrassment was negligible as compared with the risk of losing the election."[14]

America First

Even with the election safely won, however, Roosevelt could not afford to rest easy. The isolationist bloc was, if anything, growing stronger. In the fall of 1940 the America First Committee was formed. Initiated by Robert D. Stuart and a group of Yale University students, the organization quickly attracted wide support. The chairman was Gen. Robert E. Wood, a brilliant businessman and chairman of the board of Sears, Roebuck and Company. Eventually the committee claimed support from such prominent Americans as Charles A. Lindbergh, the famous aviator; John T. Flynn, a prominent journalist; William R. Castle, a former assistant secretary of state; Chester Bowles, a well-known advertising executive and public servant; Alice Roosevelt Longworth, daughter of President Theodore Roosevelt; and many others, including numerous members of Congress.[15]

Soon, opposing groups favoring intervention—such as the Committee to Defend America by Aiding the Allies, the Fight for Freedom Committee, and the Century Group[16]—were organized and waging a bitter battle of words with the America Firsters and their allies, including the No Foreign War Committee, the Keep American Out of War Congress and, until the German attack on Russia, the American Peace Mobilization, a Communist front.[17]

Into 1941 the intensity of the debate grew, as deeply felt emotions on both sides poured out. In many respects, however, it was not a fair fight. The Roosevelt Administration was committed to total support of the interventionists and its power was often used to frustrate the anti-interventionists. In 1975 hearings before Congress regarding the FBI's domestic intelligence gathering revealed that President Roosevelt often used the FBI to investigate the anti-interventionists—presumably in order to find something that could be used against them.[18] The culmination of this kind of enterprise was the infamous sedition trial of 1944. At that time, Lawrence Dennis, one of the key defendants, charged that the FBI had violated his and other isolationists' civil liberties, but in the midst of the war hysteria, no one paid much attention.[19]

The most prominent and outspoken of the prewar anti-interventionists was Charles A. Lindbergh, who was singled out for special treatment by the administration. Looking back, it is astonishing to realize to what lengths the president and the interventionists were willing to go in order to discredit him. For example, Roosevelt had Secretary of the Interior Harold Ickes organize a special cabinet committee to deal with Lindbergh. Complete files on Lindbergh's anti-interventionist speeches were kept, and Ickes made it a point to brand him as the "number one Nazi fellow traveler." Privately, the president agreed, and told Secretary of the Treasury Henry Morgenthau in 1940: "If I should die tomorrow, I want you to know this. I am absolutely convinced that Lindbergh is a Nazi."[20]

Roosevelt's Frustration

In spite of the obvious administration efforts to move closer to the world conflict—Lend-Lease, the convoying of Lend-Lease material to England and involvement of the Navy in the Battle of the Atlantic, and the occupation of Iceland and Greenland—by the fall of 1941 Roosevelt could go no further. The Neutrality Acts remained in force, and the public, while clearly favoring aid to the Allies, was steadfast in its determination to stay out of the war except in the event of a direct attack. Robert Sherwood summed up the president's frustration:

> The truth was that, as the world situation became more desperately critical, and as the limitless peril came closer and closer to the United States, isolationist sentiment became ever more strident in expression and aggressive in action, and Roosevelt was relatively powerless to combat it. He had said everything "short of war" that could be said. He had no more tricks left. The hat from which he had pulled so many rabbits was empty.[21]

At the Atlantic Conference in August 1941 Roosevelt was forced to make this reality clear to British Prime Minister Winston Churchill. They were agreed that the best hope for American entry into the war lay in provoking an incident with the Germans. But nothing could be done if Hitler would not supply one, as he had apparently decided to avoid doing.[22] Churchill related this problem to South African Prime Minister General Jan Smuts shortly after the conference:

> I do not think it would be any use for me to make a personal appeal to Roosevelt at this juncture to enter the war. At the

Atlantic meeting I told his circle that I would rather have an American declaration of war now and no supplies for six months than double the supplies and no declaration. When this was repeated to him, he thought it a hard saying. We must not underestimate his constitutional difficulties. He may take action as Chief Executive, but only Congress can declare war. He went so far as to say to me, "I may never declare war; I may make war. If I were to ask Congress to declare war, they may argue about it for three months."[23]

Back Door to War

This constitutional difficulty in bringing the United States into a war opposed by the majority of the people in the absence of a direct attack from Germany is what gave rise to the idea of a "back door to war" via Japan. Such a strategy had been enunciated by Harold Ickes early on. As he confided to his diary:

> For a long time I have believed that our best entrance into the war would be by way of Japan. . . . And, of course, if we go to war against Japan, it will inevitably lead to war against Germany.[24]

A series of provocations by the United States eventually forced the Japanese to fight for their economic survival as a nation. The most important of these was the order by Roosevelt freezing all Japanese assets in the United States, which effectively cut off all trade between the United States and Japan. The British and Dutch soon followed suit, and as a result, almost all of Japan's foreign trade was cut off. To Japan, a nation with virtually no natural resources, this action was of critical importance. In particular, Japan needed oil desperately and would have to get it one way or another, lest it suffer slow economic strangulation.[25] This trade embargo proved to be the single most important factor in eventually bringing America into actual conflict.

War Comes

On December 7, 1941, the Japanese moved to take by force that which had been denied to them through peaceful trade. The closest source of oil was in the Dutch East Indies, but the Japanese knew they could not take it without involving the British and Americans as well. Thus a first strike at the American Pacific Fleet became inevitable.

Following the attack on Pearl Harbor, many who had opposed American intervention in the war echoed America First Committee Chairman Robert Wood's statement, "Well, he got us in through the back door."[26] But with Congress' declaration of war on Japan the next day, and Germany's and Italy's declarations of war on the United States on December 11, there was nothing left for America First and the other anti-interventionist organizations to do except close up shop. America First ended its battle against intervention with this statement:

> Our principles were right. Had they been followed, war could have been avoided. No good purpose can now be served by considering what might have been, had our objectives been attained. . . . We are at war. Today, though there may be subsidiary considerations, the primary objective is . . . victory.[27]

Though the isolationists never reorganized after the war, most continued to maintain that they had been correct in opposing intervention. As Charles Lindbergh wrote many years later:

> You ask what my conclusions are . . . looking back on World War II from the vantage point of a quarter century in time. We won the war in a military sense; but in a broader sense it seems to me we lost it, for our Western civilization is less respected and secure than it was before.
> In order to defeat Germany and Japan we supported the still greater menaces of Russia and China—which now confront us in a nuclear-weapon era. Poland was not saved. The British Empire has broken down with great suffering, bloodshed and confusion. England is an economy-constricted secondary power. France had to give up her major colonies and turn into a mild dictatorship herself. Much of our Western culture was destroyed. We lost the genetic heredity formed through aeons in many million lives. Meanwhile, the Soviets have dropped their iron curtain to screen off Eastern Europe, and an antagonistic Chinese government threatens us in Asia.
> More than a generation after the war's end, our occupying armies still must occupy, and the world has not been made safe for democracy and freedom. On the contrary, our system of democratic government is being challenged by that greatest

of dangers to any government: internal dissatisfaction and unrest.

It is alarmingly possible that World War II marks the beginning of our Western civilization's breakdown, as it already marks the breakdown of the greatest empire ever built by man. Certainly our civilization's survival depends on meeting the challenges that tower before us with unprecedented magnitude in almost every field of modern life. Most of these challenges were, at least, intensified through the waging of World War II.[28]

It is in this context that we must examine the origins of Pearl Harbor and the subsequent investigations. The issue is much broader than the matter of whether or not the Pearl Harbor attack could have been prevented. It calls into question a vast number of assumptions about foreign policy and America's role in the world that were set in place on December 7, 1941, and which have major implications for today. Pearl Harbor meant not only the needless deaths of 2,403 American fighting men, but ultimately the deaths of the balance of power in Europe and Asia and of American neutrality.

Because the United States was forced to fill the power vacuums created by the decline of Germany, Italy, Japan, Great Britain, and France as world powers, lest the void be filled by communism, American security is now believed to depend upon worldwide political stability. Every power vacuum is now hotly contested by the Communist regimes and the United States, even though the areas and issues involved may have no tangible importance to the United States.

Prior to World War II it was possible to assume that America's legitimate interests extended only to those matters that directly affected the continental United States. It was possible to ignore the problems of Europe, Asia, and Africa and not fear for American security. Pearl Harbor destroyed that because the ultimate guilt was placed not upon those responsible for provoking and instigating the attack, but upon isolationism. If it were not for isolationism, it was—and is—said, the United States would have been prepared. This is nonsense.

If one believes that American neutrality is still a desirable position, one must first destroy the myths of the past. It must be made clear that Pearl Harbor happened not because the United States was noninterventionist but because of specific actions by specific individuals. Only then can the consequences of World War II be examined with an eye to what might have been. If one then concludes that things would have been worse had the U.S. not intervened in the war, he will probably say that, all things considered, Pearl Harbor was a small price to pay. But if he believes that things could not possibly be worse and that they might have been much better, Pearl Harbor takes on a very different meaning, with great implications for American policy even today. This is why the Pearl Harbor episode is still important, almost four decades after the bombs began to fall on that fateful Sunday morning.

2

Origins of American Involvement in the War, Part 1

President Roosevelt took his first concrete step toward war at the end of 1937 when he sent Capt. Royal E. Ingersoll to London to arrange for "parallel action in the Far East." It was Ingersoll's mission to get British opinion regarding the freezing of Japanese assets and to inform the British that Roosevelt had decided to renounce the London Treaty on naval arms and press ahead for more and bigger ships.[1] The assumption of the trip was that both Great Britain and the United States would eventually find themselves at war with Japan at the same time and would need to coordinate command relationships. It should be noted that despite the worsening European situation the entire thrust of the trip was action against Japan.[2] In many ways the trip foreshadowed later military and naval staff meetings that culminated in the so-called ADB agreements with the Dutch and British, which set forth the contingencies under which war with Japan would occur.

Interestingly, at this same time Roosevelt also sent Joseph Davies to the Soviet Union on a similar mission. As Davies later reported:

> In January 1938, and prior to my departure for the Soviet Union, the President directed me to explore the possibility of securing a liaison between the military and naval authorities of the United States and the Soviet Union with a view to the inter-change of information as to the facts with reference to the military and naval situations of the United States and the Soviet Union vis-à-vis Japan and the general Far Eastern and Pacific problem.[3]

The War in Europe

With the outbreak of war in Europe on September 1, 1939, Churchill sought to enlist American intervention. To this end he wrote to President Roosevelt suggesting that they set up a system of private communication. Churchill, because he was still first lord of the admiralty at the time, called himself "Former Naval Person" in these communications, while Roosevelt used the code name "POTUS" (President of the United States). Of these communications Churchill was later to say, "My relations with the President gradually became so close that the chief business between our two countries was virtually conducted by these personal interchanges between him and me."[4]

The secret of what was contained in these communications has fascinated historians for more than thirty years. Some have speculated that Roosevelt and Churchill were secretly plotting American entry into the war. This suspicion has been reinforced over the years by the case of Tyler Kent, the code clerk in the American embassy in London who read and stole copies of the Roosevelt-Churchill correspondence. In May 1940 Kent was arrested by British police for violation of the Official Secrets Act.[5]

Declassification of the relevant documents, however, now makes it clear that no such plot existed. Copies of all documents in Kent's possession at the time of his arrest are now available, as is the complete correspondence between Roosevelt and Churchill. As tempting as it is to believe that there are secret messages left to be discovered, it must be concluded none exist.[6] This is not to say, of course, that the disclosure of a Roosevelt-Churchill correspondence, before Churchill became prime minister, would not have been of vast importance had it been known. Indeed, had Kent been able to smuggle his documents back to the United States it would have created a furor of the first order, for no matter how innocent the correspondence may seem today, public disclosure of Roosevelt's massive unneutrality might have denied him reelection in 1940.

The Fall of France

By late spring 1940, the situation in Europe was becoming critical. On May 10 German armies advanced into France and by June 9 the French government was evacuating Paris. On June 14 Churchill told French Prime Minister Paul Reynaud:

> If France . . . continues in the field and in the war, we feel that the United States is committed beyond recall to take the only remaining step, namely, becoming a belligerent in form as she already has constituted herself in fact. The Constitution of the United States makes it impossible, as you foresaw, for the President to declare war himself, but . . . we sincerely believe that this must inevitably follow.[7]

Of course Roosevelt could not openly commit the United States to military involvement the war; Congress would never approve. But in spite of that, Churchill continued to press Roosevelt at every opportunity to become an actual belligerent. Toward this end, he threatened that the British fleet might be lost if America did not come into the war. Roosevelt had naturally assumed that even if England fell, the fleet would remain intact within the Commonwealth. Lord Lothian, the British ambassador to the United States, informed the president that this was not necessarily true. It was possible, he said, that the fleet may destroy itself in a suicide attack on German ports.[8]

Churchill himself made this clear in a letter to Roosevelt on June 15, 1940:

> Although the present Government and I personally would never fail to send the fleet across the Atlantic if resistance was beaten down here, a point may be reached in the struggle where the present Ministers no longer have control of affairs and when very easy terms could be obtained for the British Islands by their becoming a vassal state of the Hitler empire. A pro-German Government would certainly be called into being to make peace and might present to a shattered or starving nation an almost irresistable case for entire submission to the Nazi will. The fate of the British Fleet, as I have already mentioned to you, would be decisive on the future of the United States because, if it were joined to the fleets of Japan, France, and Italy and the great resources of German industry, over-

whelming sea-power would be in Hitler's hands. . . . If we go down, you may have a United States of Europe under the Nazi command far more numerous, far stronger, far better armed than the New World.[9]

This would have entirely upset the historic relationship that gave the British navy responsibility for patrolling the Atlantic while the U.S. Navy guarded the Pacific. It would force the United States to divide its fleet in half, inferior to the Japanese in the Pacific and vulnerable to the Germans in the Atlantic. This "threat" is further evidence that the British would go to any lengths to bring the United States into the war.

Britain and the "Back Door"

While doing their best to get American intervention in Europe, the British also sought to force the United States to take a more aggressive posture in the Far East. They hoped that the United States could be induced to protect British possessions in the Far East from encroachment by Japan. In effect, the British wanted the United States to safeguard their Asian empire for them. As Lord Lothian was told in June 1940:

> The collapse of France would provide Japan with the temptation to take action against French, British or Dutch interests in the Far East. We see no hope of being able to dispatch a fleet to Singapore. It will therefore be vital that the United States of America should publicly declare her intention to regard any alteration of the *status quo* in the Far East and the Pacific as a *casus belli*. [10]

The British believed that when the United States finally entered the war it would be against Japan rather than Germany. But they feared that this might not lead to American intervention in Europe and that the United States would become preoccupied in the Pacific to the point of abandoning England. Thus the British were overjoyed when the Tripartite Agreement between Germany, Italy and Japan was announced. This assured that if the U.S. went to war with Japan it would also go to war against Germany.[11]

In addition to making threats about destroying their fleet and provoking a confrontation in the Far East, the British sought to

27

bring economic pressure on the United States. This Churchill attempted in a letter to Roosevelt on December 8, 1940:

> The moment approaches when we shall no longer be able to pay cash for shipping and other supplies. While we will do our utmost, and shrink from no proper sacrifice to make payments across the Exchange, I believe you will agree that it would be wrong in principle and mutually disadvantageous in effect if, at the height of this struggle, Great Britain were to be divested of all saleable assets so that after the victory was won with our blood, civilisation saved, and the time gained for the United States to be fully armed against all eventualities, we should stand stripped to the bone. Such a course would not be in the moral or economic interests of either of our countries. We here would be unable, after the war, to purchase the large balance of imports which is agreeable to your tariffs and industrial economy. Not only should we in Great Britain suffer cruel privations but widespread unemployment in the United States would follow the curtailment of American exporting power.[12]

This was not an idle threat, for American policy-makers were already concerned about what would happen to the American economy when the war ended. They knew that despite all the New Deal programs it was the war in Europe that ended the Great Depression, and they feared that without war orders to pump up the economy depression would start up again where it had left off.[13]

Lend-Lease

Roosevelt's response to the British financial plight was Lend-Lease. This measure was introduced in January 1941, and passed by Congress in March. The initial appropriation was for $7 billion, and before the war ended more than $50 billion had been appropriated.[14]

Such a massive investment in the British war effort could not fail to have important consequences for the United States. Thenceforth the U.S. would have a tangible vested interest in the outcome of the war and could no longer be considered a neutral. This fact was recognized by everyone involved, despite the administration's claim that Lend-Lease would make American intervention unnecessary. Thus Richard Leopold has written in *The Growth of American Foreign Policy:* "The Lend-Lease Act of March 11, 1941, drove the final nail into the coffin of neutrality."[15]

Immediately after passage of Lend-Lease, the president moved quickly to expand its scope through convoys. He argued, quite logically, that it made no sense to give the British aid if we were not prepared to guarantee its delivery. Opponents argued, equally logically, that the United States was inviting an incident that would lead to a shooting war.[16]

On April 9 Roosevelt moved to expand still further American involvement in the world crisis by signing an agreement with Denmark that included Greenland in "our sphere of hemispheric defense." A similar agreement with Iceland was signed in July, leading to American occupation of that island nation.

Throughout all this the Germans proved themselves remarkably restrained and would not give the president an incident to justify further American intervention. Then, on September 4, an American destroyer, the U.S.S. *Greer,* was attacked by a German submarine off the coast of Iceland. Roosevelt immediately seized upon the issue to adopt a new, more highly provocative stance toward Germany. The president said the *Greer* was carrying American mail to Iceland and was attacked without warning, although she was in international waters flying the American flag. Henceforth, he said, American ships had orders to shoot German submarines on sight.[17] Unfortunately, the truth of the incident was a good bit different.

The truth came out a few weeks later when Adm. Harold Stark, chief of naval operations, disclosed that the *Greer* had been informed by British aircraft that a German submarine was about ten miles ahead. The *Greer* gave chase for more than three hours, during which time the submarine fired two torpedoes and the *Greer* responded with depth charges. Eventually, contact with the submarine was lost and the *Greer* went on to Iceland.[18]

A few weeks later another American warship, the U.S.S. *Kearny,* was attacked and damaged by a German submarine. On October 27 the president told the country: "We have wished to avoid shooting. But the shooting has started. And history has recorded who fired the first shot. In the long run, however, all that will matter is who fired the last shot. America has been attacked."[19]

When the truth of the *Kearny* incident finally came out, it became clear that Germany had not fired the first shot at all. Like the

29

Greer, the *Kearny* had sighted the German sub and fired first. The result was that the American people refused to become inflamed by the incident. Thus when the first American ship, the U.S.S. *Reuben James,* was actually sunk on October 30, the president did not make much of it.[20]

Japan Hopes for Peace

As early as 1939 Japan had no doubt that the United States was becoming antagonistic toward her and that war was on the horizon. On May 18, 1939, the Japanese prime minister and the minister for foreign affairs sought to ease the tensions with a far-ranging peace proposal. Their proposal read, in part:

> At present there is a serious antagonism among the nations of Europe and no one can assure that there will be no clash in the near future. If, by mischance, war is to break out, its consequences would be practically beyond our imagination and the indescribable sufferings of hundreds of millions of people as well as complete destruction of civilization would ensue. It is, therefore, absolutely necessary for us to exert our effort to prevent the occurrence of such catastrophe, and, I believe, that is the duty mainly incumbent on the United States and Japan since these two powers are situated outside the scope of European conflict. . . . Undoubtedly the intention of the United States Government is to prevent the occurrence of such catastrophe and thus to save Europe from the misery of war. Similarly it is the ardent wish of Japan that nations should have their own proper places in the world and thus the true world peace might be established and maintained. I, for myself, am doing my utmost to realize this ideal, and on this point, I believe, will be found the possibility of much closer co-operation between Japan and America as well as the foundation of a deeper mutual understanding between the two nations.[21]

The Japanese prime minister also said "that this might prove to be the last opportunity to save the world from chaos."[22]

The sincerity of this proposal was not lost upon Secretary of State Cordell Hull, who observed, "This is, in effect, a private *demarche* of the Prime Minister to us."[23] But Roosevelt chose to ignore the overture and instead spoke of sanctions against Japan.

Sanctions Against Japan

Ambassador Joseph Grew, the American ambassador to Japan, was perplexed by the president's attitude and confused as to why his recommendations for a more moderate position toward Japan were ignored. After the Pearl Harbor attack, when diplomacy had been relegated to the battlefield, Grew confided to his diary:

> Our own telegrams brought no response whatsoever; they were never even referred to, and reporting to the Department was like throwing pebbles into a lake at night; we were not permitted to see even the ripples. For all we knew our telegrams had not in any degree registered. Obviously I could only assume our recommendations were not welcome, yet we continued to express our carefully considered judgement as to the developing situation, a judgement which subsequent events proved to have been all too accurate.[24]

Later Grew would blame Stanley Hornbeck, the State Department's Far East advisor, for withholding his telegrams from Secretary Hull.[25] It is clear that there was more to the matter than this, however, because it was the president who was directing American foreign policy toward Japan.[26]

As early as June 1938, the U.S. government had begun what was called a "moral embargo" on goods to Japan both by discouraging private companies from shipping certain goods to Japan, notably airplanes and airplane parts, and by dissuading American financial interests from extending credits to Japanese enterprises.[27]

At the time, the provisions of our Treaty of Commerce and Navigation with Japan prevented any overt attempt to place an embargo on Japan, unless similar action were taken against all other countries at the same time. This treaty also provided that six months' notice be given before the treaty could be abrogated by either side. On July 26, 1939, the United States gave notice that the treaty would expire effective January 26, 1940, with the probability that sanctions would soon follow.[28]

Ambassador Grew was in Washington when this happened and he discussed the situation with Roosevelt. In his diary he wrote:

> Officially I obtained the usual modicum of information but very seldom is one able to get a clear-cut definition of policy or any definition of policy except in broad and general terms. There is however an unmistakable hardening of the Adminis-

tration's attitude toward Japan and a marked disinclination to allow American interests to be crowded out of China. In both my talks with the President I brought out clearly my view that if we once start sanctions against Japan we must see them through to the end, and the end may conceivably be war. I also said that if we cut off Japan's supply of oil and if Japan then finds that she cannot obtain sufficient oil from other commercial sources to ensure her national security, she will in all probability send her fleet down to take the Dutch East Indies. The President replied significantly: "Then we could easily intercept her fleet." Meanwhile we have denounced our Treaty of 1911 and have sent several extra ships and planes to Pearl Harbor and to Manila. I think it is going to be up to me to let this American temper discreetly penetrate into Japanese consciousness. Sparks may well fly before long. . . .[29]

The Embargo Begins

On July 2, 1940, President Roosevelt signed into law the Export Control Act, which empowered him to prohibit the export of munitions, materials, and machinery essential to the national defense. The same day, he acted under that authority to prohibit the export of all arms and munitions, numerous chemicals and raw materials, aircraft parts, armor plate, and various kinds of metalworking machinery to any country. Later in July this order was expanded to include aviation fuel, lubricants, and heavy melting iron.[30] In view of her reliance on such materials, Japan believed she "had been singled out for and subjected to discriminatory treatment."[31] She protested vigorously.

On September 26 the president expanded his order to prohibit the export to Japan of all grades of iron and steel scrap. Once again, the Japanese protested:

In view of the fact that Japan has been for some years the principal buyer of American iron and steel scrap, the announcement of the administrative policy, as well as the regulations establishing a license system in iron and steel scrap cannot fail to be regarded as directed against Japan, and, as such, to be an unfriendly act. . . . In view of the high feeling in Japan it is apprehended that, in the event of continuation by the United States Government of the present attitude toward Japan in matters of trade restriction, especially if it leads to the imposition of further measures of curtailment, future relations between Japan and the United States will be unpredictable.[32]

On October 10, 1940, Adm. James O. Richardson, commander-in-chief, Pacific Fleet (CINCPAC), went to see President Roosevelt to discuss what the American reaction would be should the Japanese respond to the American embargo by seizing the materials they needed. As Richardson related the conversation:

> In the event the Japanese took drastic action, he, the President, was considering shutting off all trade between Japan and the Americas, and to this end was considering establishing a patrol of light ships in two lines extending from Hawaii westward to the Philippines, and from Samoa toward the Dutch East Indies. I was amazed at the proposal and stated that the fleet was not prepared to put such a plan into effect, nor for the war which would certainly result from such a course of action, and that we would certainly lose many ships.[33]

Richardson went on to say that the fleet was very inadequately prepared for war and that there was an immediate need for more personnel and better training. When Roosevelt told him that this was not possible, Richardson said to him: "Mr. President, I feel that I must tell you that the senior officers of the Navy do not have the trust and confidence in the civilian leadership of this country that is essential for the successful prosecution of a war in the Pacific." To which the president replied, "Joe, you just don't understand that this is an election year and there are certain things that can't be done, no matter what, until the election is over and won."[34]

The Pacific Fleet

Historically, the U.S. Pacific Fleet had been based on the West Coast, primarily at San Diego. In May 1940, however, the fleet was ordered on maneuvers to Pearl Harbor, Hawaii. This was to have been a routine training mission of short duration, but within a short time Admiral Richardson was given orders extending the fleet's stay in Hawaii indefinitely. Richardson became concerned about this change in the fleet's operating base because of the lack of proper facilities at Pearl Harbor. He therefore wrote to Chief of

Naval Operations Stark requesting a definite answer as to why the fleet was in Hawaii and how long it would stay there.[35] This is Stark's reply:

Why are you in the Hawaiian area?
Answer: You are there because of the deterrent effect which it is thought your presence may have on the Japs going into the East Indies. In previous letters I have hooked this up with the Italians going into the war. The connection is that with Italy in, it is thought the Japs might feel just that much freer to take independent action. We believe both the Germans and the Italians have told the Japs that so far as they are concerned she, Japan, has a free hand in the Dutch East Indies. . . . The above I think will answer the question "why you are there." It does not answer the question as to how long you will stay. Rest assured that the minute I get this information I will communicate it to you. Nobody can answer it just now. Like you, I have asked that question, and also—like you—I have been unable to get the answer.[36]

Throughout the rest of 1940 Richardson pressed for return of the fleet to California. As he put it in one dispatch: "If the disposition of the Fleet were determined solely by Naval considerations, the major portion of the fleet should return to its normal Pacific Coast bases because such basing would facilitate its training and its preparation for war."[37] But the fleet stayed at Pearl Harbor.

In January 1941 Richardson was notified that as of February 1 he was relieved of his command of the Pacific Fleet, to be replaced by Adm. Husband E. Kimmel. Richardson was understandably upset at this change, which cut short a normal tour of duty. Back in Washington, he questioned Secretary of the Navy Frank Knox about the premature change in command and was told: "Why, Richardson, when you were here in Washington last October, you hurt the President's feelings by what you said to him. You should realize that. But, I am sure that some day soon, the President will send for you and have a talk." Needless to say, the president never called.[38]

The Strategy for War

The same month that Admiral Richardson was relieved of his command, British and American military and naval staffs met in Washington under strict secrecy to plot an overall strategy for the war—a war in which the United States was not yet a belligerent. The basis for these staff meetings was summarized in their final report:

> The Staff Conference assumes that when the United States becomes involved in war with Germany, it will at the same time engage in war with Italy. In these circumstances, the possibility of a state of war arising between Japan and an Association of the United States, the British Commonwealth and its Allies, including the Netherlands East Indies, must be taken into account.[39]

The secrecy of these talks was so great that the British delegation wore disguises.[40] This was not so much to protect them from being discovered by the Germans or Japanese but by American newspapers! For the fact is that the presence of British military officers holding talks with American military officers at this time would have been further evidence of the administration's interventionist leanings. Thus Robert Sherwood noted:

> It is an ironic fact that in all probability no great damage would have been done had the details of these plans fallen into the hands of the Germans and the Japanese; whereas, had they fallen into the hands of the Congress and the press, American preparation for war might have been well nigh wreaked and ruined.[41]

As a result of these talks, American war plans were completely rewritten to reflect the new strategy. The agreement reached with the British, known as ABC-1, was incorporated into the Navy's basic war plan as Rainbow No. 5. Rainbow 5 was relayed in turn to Admiral Kimmel in the form of War Plan Pac46, or WPPac46, which governed all fleet operations in the Pacific upon the outbreak of war.[42] In his letter to Admiral Kimmel informing him of the new plan, Admiral Stark said:

> The question as to our entry into the war now seems to be *when,* and not *whether.* Public opinion, which now is slowly turning in that direction, may or may not be accelerated. My

own personal view is that we may be in the war (possibly undeclared) against Germany and Italy within about two months but that there is a reasonable possibility that Japan may remain out altogether. However, we cannot at present act on that possibility.[43]

The ABC-1 was further amplified in April 1941 by meetings between American, Dutch, and British military and naval staffs in Singapore. They produced an agreement along the lines of ABC-1 known as ADB. The most important part of this agreement was that it set geographical limits beyond which the Japanese would not be allowed to go. The plan outlined five contingencies under which war would take place:

    (a) A direct attack by Japanese forces against the territory of any of the three powers.
    (b) The movement of Japanese forces into any part of Thailand to the West of 100° East or to the South of 10° North.
    (c) The movement of Japanese warships toward the Philippines, the East coast of the Isthmus of Kra or the East coast of Malaya, or across the parallel of 6° North.
    (d) The movement of Japanese forces into Portuguese Timor.
    (e) The movement of Japanese forces into New Caledonia or the Loyalty Islands.[44]

It would seem, therefore, that the United States was obligated to declare war even in the absence of a direct attack on American territory. Indeed, it would seem that the United States was obliged to declare war *even in the absence of any attack at all,* if the Japanese merely crossed a geographic boundary situated west of 100 degrees east or south of 10 degrees north.[45]

"Shoot on Sight"

The possibility that war might actually open other than because of a direct attack on American territory was never taken seriously, because it was believed that Hitler would certainly provide a suitable provocation in due time. Such an incident was expected any time after Lend-Lease was approved. As Roosevelt later told Churchill, "If the Germans did not like it they could attack American forces."[46] But the Germans refused to provide an adequate *casus belli,* even after Roosevelt gave orders for ships convoying

Lend-Lease aid to shoot German submarines on sight. Churchill reported to his cabinet the motive for this order: "Everything was to be done to force an incident."[47]

Unfortunately, Churchill and Roosevelt did not reckon with Hitler's resolve to keep America out of the war, so as not to repeat Germany's error of World War I. The strength of this resolve was observed by the Italian foreign minister, Count Galeazzo Ciano, while on a visit to German General Headquarters. In his diary he wrote: "The Germans have firmly decided to do nothing which will accelerate or cause America's entry into the war."[48]

The problem of how to get the United States into the war came to a head at the Atlantic Conference. Churchill pressed Roosevelt for an immediate declaration of war and told him that he would rather have a declaration of war and no supplies for six months than twice the supplies and no declaration. To this Roosevelt replied, "I may never declare war; I may make war. If I were to ask Congress to declare war they may argue about it for three months."[49] This was the best Churchill could get, but he returned to England convinced of the "astonishing depth of Roosevelt's intense desire for war."[50]

Responding to Churchill's urgings that something be done to force the war issue in the Pacific, Roosevelt agreed to send an ultimatum to Japan in an effort to produce a *casus belli*. He and Churchill drafted a note for this purpose, which said: "Any further encroachment by Japan in the Southwest Pacific would produce a situation in which the United States Government would be compelled to take counter-measures, even though these might lead to war between the United States and Japan."[51]

The Atlantic Charter itself was to serve as an ultimatum to Germany. Churchill later commented on the significance of the charter in this respect:

> The profound and far-reaching importance of this Joint Declaration was apparent. The fact alone of the United States, still technically neutral, joining with a belligerent power in making such a declaration was astonishing. The inclusion in it of a reference to "the final destruction of the Nazi tyranny" amounted to a challenge which in ordinary times would have implied warlike action.[52]

When Churchill returned to England he told Parliament what had transpired: "I discussed . . . with Mr. Roosevelt, that the

United States, even if not herself attacked, would come into a war in the Far East, and thus make final victory sure. . . . As time went on, one had greater assurances that if Japan ran amok in the Pacific, we would not fight alone."[53]

The Freeze Order

On July 25, 1941, Roosevelt ordered all Japanese assets in the United States frozen, thus effectively ending all trade between the countries.[54] The British and Dutch followed suit. Historian Robert J. C. Butow likened the situation in Japan to that of a man who has just had a noose placed around his neck.[55] Under such circumstances a desperate act might seem like the only way out. Thus Langer and Gleason later concluded, "The freezing order was probably the crucial step in the entire course of Japanese-American relations before Pearl Harbor."[56]

Interestingly, just six days before the president's action, Adm. Richmond Kelly Turner, Navy chief of war plans, had prepared a report for him on the probable consequences of imposing an oil embargo on Japan. Turner's report said in part:

It is generally believed that shutting off the American supply of petroleum will lead promptly to an invasion of the Netherlands East Indies. . . . An embargo on exports will have an immediate severe psychological reaction in Japan against the United States. It is almost certain to intensify the determination of those now in power to continue their present course. Furthermore, it seems certain that, if Japan should then take military measures against the British and Dutch, she would also include military action against the Philippines, which would immediately involve us in a Pacific war.[57]

The recommendation of the report was "that trade with Japan not be embargoed at this time."[58] Admiral Stark then wrote on the report, "I concur in general," and passed it on to the president. Stark later told Sumner Welles, "The President expressed himself as pleased with it."[59] Thus the conclusion is unavoidable that Roosevelt's action was taken with full regard to the probable consequences.

The day before the freezing order, Roosevelt gave Japanese Ambassador Adm. Kichisaburo Nomura a warning:

The President said that if Japan attempted to seize oil supplies by force in the Netherlands East Indies, the Dutch would, without a doubt, resist, the British would immediately come to their assistance, war would then result between Japan, the British, and the Dutch, and, in view of our own policy of assisting Great Britain, an exceedingly serious situation would immediately result.[60]

This made it clear to the Japanese that the United States was allied with the British and Dutch and that they were united in their efforts to crush Japanese "ambitions."

Following the announcement that Japanese assets were being frozen, the Japanese government sent the following message to its embassies in Washington and Berlin:

Commercial and economic relations between Japan and third countries, led by England and the United States, are gradually becoming so horribly strained that we cannot endure it much longer. Consequently, our Empire, to save its very life, must take measures to secure the raw materials of the South Seas. Our Empire must immediately take steps to break asunder this ever-strengthening chain of encirclement which is being woven under the guidance and with the participation of England and the United States, acting like a cunning dragon seemingly asleep.[61]

Soon thereafter, in August 1941, a somber Ambassador Grew recorded in his diary:

The vicious circle of reprisals and counter reprisals is on. . . . Unless radical surprises occur in the world, it is difficult to see how the momentum of the down-grade movement can be arrested, or how far it will go. The obvious conclusion is eventual war.[62]

The Proposed Meeting with Konoye

Perhaps the last hope of heading off war was the proposal for a meeting between President Roosevelt and Prince Fumimaro Konoye, the Japanese prime minister. The proposal for such a meeting was made to Ambassador Grew on August 18 by Japanese Minister for Foreign Affairs Teijiro Toyoda. In his report to the State Department regarding this meeting Grew said:

Needless to say the Premier's going abroad would have no precedent in Japanese history and the Prime Minister, Prince Konoye, has made up his mind with an extremely strong determination to meet the President notwithstanding the fact that he is fully aware of the objections in certain parts of this country [Japan]. This determination of Prince Konoye is nothing but the expression of his strongest desire to save the civilization of the world from ruin as well as to maintain peace in the Pacific by making every effort in his power, and the Minister firmly believes that the President will also be in harmony with this thought and will give his consent to the proposal of the Japanese Government. . . . The Ambassador urges, however, with all the force at his command, for the sake of avoiding the obviously growing possibility of an utterly futile war between Japan and the United States, that this Japanese proposal not be turned aside without very prayerful consideration. Not only is the proposal unprecedented in Japanese history, but is an indication that Japanese intransigence is not crystallized completely owing to the fact that the proposal has the approval of the Emperor and the highest authorities in the land. The good which may flow from a meeting between Prince Konoye and President Roosevelt is incalculable. The opportunity is here presented, the Ambassador ventures to believe, for an act of the highest statesmanship, such as the recent meeting of President Roosevelt with Prime Minister Churchill at sea, with the possible overcoming thereby of apparently insurmountable obstacles to peace hereafter in the Pacific.[63]

The proposed meeting with Konoye never took place, because Roosevelt and the State Department saw it as merely a delaying tactic.[64] Soon thereafter Konoye's moderate government fell from power and was replaced by the war party headed by Gen. Hideki Tojo. This was clearly a turn for the worse as far as chances for peace were concerned.

Grew continued his warnings about the consequences of American policy toward Japan, but to no avail. As Herbert Feis notes: "The incoming reports from Grew were somber and his diary even more so. War, they said, was near unless the American government granted a reprieve by relaxing economic restraints."[65]

On November 3, 1941, Grew sent his strongest warning yet:

It would be shortsighted for American policy to be based upon the belief that Japanese preparations are no more than saber rattling, merely intended to give moral support to the high diplomacy of Japan. Action by Japan which might render unavoidable an armed conflict with the United States may come with dangerous and dramatic suddenness.[66]

In spite of this, Hull continued to press the Japanese hard on every point, particularly about Japan's alliance with Germany, although Ambassador Grew had made it clear

that in regard specifically to Japan's Axis relations, the Japanese Government, though refusing consistently to give an undertaking that it will overtly renounce its alliance membership, actually has shown a readiness to reduce Japan's alliance adherence to a dead letter by its indication of willingness to enter formally into negotiations with the United States."[67]

3

Origins of American Involvement in the War, Part 2

The reason that Roosevelt could be complacent about the Japanese threat was in part due to the fact that his knowledge about Japan's intentions was being supplemented by an amazing source: Japan's own top secret diplomatic correspondence.

The Japanese secret diplomatic code was first broken by Herbert O. Yardley in the 1920s. This helped Secretary of State Charles Evans Hughes immeasurably during the naval treaty negotiations of 1921–22.[1] The ability to read the Japanese code was lost when Secretary of State Henry L. Stimson closed Yardley's operation, known as the Black Chamber, in 1929 with the admonition: "Gentlemen do not read each other's mail."[2] In the 1930s the Japanese developed a new code system based on totally new concepts. This new code was called "Purple," and the Japanese believed it to be absolutely unbreakable.

Eventually it was realized that codebreaking was an important part of intelligence and a new effort was made to break the Japanese diplomatic code. For many months the Army's chief cryptologist, William F. Friedman, worked steadily on the Purple Code without success, until one day in August 1940 when Harry Clark, one of Friedman's assistants, hit upon the key to breaking the code. Utilizing Clark's insight Friedman was able to crack the Purple Code within a short time.[3]

The breaking of the Purple Code was an achievement of incredible proportions. Not only was the code broken, but a working copy of the Purple Code machine was built. This made it possible for the United States to read Japan's diplomatic messages with amazing speed. Extra machines were manufactured, and a regular procedure for intercepting, decrypting, translating, evaluating, and distributing Japanese diplomatic correspondence was set up. The intercepted and decoded Japanese messages, dubbed "Magic," were soon being read by many top government officials, including the president, the secretaries of state, war and navy, the army chief of staff and the chief of naval operations. In addition, as many as three Purple Code machines (out of a total of eight manufactured) were given to the British, although none was ever sent to Pearl Harbor.[4]

With the knowledge that American policy-makers were able to read Japan's most secret diplomatic messages, a new light is shed upon American policy toward Japan from 1940 onward. No longer can we simply assume that the provocations against Japan were merely shortsighted. We must assume that President Roosevelt and the State Department knew precisely what they were doing and knew that war would be the result.

The Japanese Intercepts

The information obtained from the broken Japanese code was of enormous diplomatic and military value. Since the Japanese had no idea that the Americans were reading their top secret correspondence, the content of this correspondence can be taken as a reflection of authentic Japanese views. Thus it would serve either as a check on the sincerity of Japanese peace overtures, or as a proof of their treachery. By and large, the intercepts provide support for the view that the Japanese sincerely wanted peace but were provoked by U.S. officials making unreasonable demands. For example, on November 4, 1941, Tokyo sent the following long message to its ambassador in Washington:

> Well, relations between Japan and the United States have reached the edge, and our people are losing confidence in the possibility of ever adjusting them. . . . Conditions both within and without our Empire are so tense that no longer is procrastination possible, yet in our sincerity to maintain pacific relationships between the Empire of Japan and the United States of America, we have decided, as a result of these deliberations, to gamble once more on the countinuance of the parleys, but this is our last effort. Both in name and spirit this counter-proposal of ours is, indeed, the last. I want you to know that. If through it we do not reach a quick accord, I am

sorry to say the talks will certainly be ruptured. Then, indeed, will relations between our two nations be on the brink of chaos. I mean that the success or failure of the pending discussions will have an immense effect on the destiny of the Empire of Japan. In fact, we gambled the fate of our land on the throw of this die.

When the Japanese-American meetings began, who would have ever dreamt that they would drag out so long? Hoping that we could fast come to some understanding, we have already gone far out of our way and yielded and yielded. The United States does not appreciate this, but through thick and thin sticks to the self-same propositions she made to start with. Those of our people and of our officials who suspect the sincerity of the Americans are far from few. Bearing all kinds of humiliating things our Government has repeatedly stated its sincerity and gone far, yes, too far, in giving in to them. There is just one reason why we do this—to maintain peace in the Pacific. There seem to be some Americans who think we would make a one-sided deal, but our temperance, I can tell you, has not come from weakness, and naturally there is an end to our long suffering. Nay, when it comes to a question of our existence and our honor, when the time comes we will defend them without recking [*sic*] the cost. If the United States takes an attitude that overlooks or shuns this position of ours, there is not a whit of use in ever broaching the talks. This time we are showing the limit of our friendship; this time we are making our last possible bargain, and I hope that we can thus settle all our troubles with the United States peaceably.[5]

The message went on to spell out several concessions the Japanese were willing to make on the issue of Japanese troops stationed in China and Indochina. These concessions were delivered to Secretary of State Hull on November 7.[6] Hull already knew what to expect from having read the intercept of the Japanese message containing the proposals.[7] Despite this knowledge, earlier in the day he had told a cabinet meeting that "relations are extremely critical. We should be on the lookout for a military attack by Japan anywhere at any time."[8] Of course Hull also knew that the Japanese had sent with their first proposal a second proposal containing greater concessions.[9] It was a simple matter to sit back and wait for them to be offered.

Shortly after receipt of the message containing the new Japanese peace proposals, a message was received setting a deadline for conclusion of the peace talks. On November 5 Tokyo sent this message to Ambassador Nomura in Washington:

> Because of various circumstances, it is absolutely necessary that all arrangements for the signing of this agreement be completed by the 25th of this month. I realize that this is a difficult order, but under the circumstances it is an unavoidable one. Please understand this thoroughly and tackle the problem of saving the Japanese-U.S. relations from falling into a chaotic condition. Do so with great determination and with unstinted effort, I beg of you.[10]

Hull later recalled that when he saw this message it "could mean only one thing. Japan had already set in motion the wheels of her war machine, and she had decided not to stop short of war with the United States if by November 25 we had not agreed to her demands."[11]

The Modus Vivendi

Though Hull may have had good reason to believe that the Japanese proposals were inadequate, it might have been more prudent for him to have at least led the Japanese along for a while instead of casually dismissing their proposals. If his purpose was to provoke the Japanese into an attack, such would at least have given the U.S. time to build up its forces. This was the idea behind the *modus vivendi* proposed by Admiral Stark and Army Chief of Staff Gen. George C. Marshall on November 5. In a memorandum to the president, they made the following points:

> At the present time the United States Fleet in the Pacific is inferior to the Japanese Fleet and cannot undertake an unlimited strategic offensive in the Western Pacific. In order to be able to do so, it would have to be strengthened by withdrawing practically all naval vessels from the Atlantic except those assigned to local defense forces. . . .
> The current plans for war against Japan in the Far East are to conduct defensive war, in cooperation with the British and Dutch, for the defense of the Philippines and the British and Dutch East Indies. The Philippines are now being reinforced. The present combined naval, air, and ground forces will make attack on the islands a hazardous undertaking. By about the

middle of December, 1941, United States air and submarine strength in the Philippines will have become a positive threat to any Japanese operations south of Formosa. The U.S. Army air forces in the Philippines will have reached the projected strength by February or March, 1942. The potency of this threat will have then increased to a point where it might well be a deciding factor in deterring Japan in operations in the areas south and west of the Philippines. By this time, additional British naval and air reinforcements to Singapore will have arrived. The general defensive strength of the entire southern area against possible Japanese operations will then have reached impressive proportions. . . .

The Chief of Naval Operations and the Chief of Staff are in accord in the following conclusions:

(a) The basic military policies and strategy agreed to in the United States-British Staff conversations remain sound. . . .

(b) War between the United States and Japan should be avoided while building up defensive forces in the Far East, until such time as Japan attacks or directly threatens territories whose security to the United States is of very great importance. Military action against Japan should be undertaken only in one of the following contingencies:

(1) A direct act of war by Japanese armed forces against the territory or mandated territory of the United States, the British Commonwealth, or the Netherlands East Indies;

(2) The movement of Japanese forces into Thailand to the west of 100° East or South of 10° North; or into Portuguese Timor, New Caledonia, or the Loyalty Islands.

(c) If war with Japan cannot be avoided, it should follow the strategic lines of existing war plans; i.e., military operations should be primarily defensive, with the object of holding territory, and weakening Japan's economic position.

(d) Considering world strategy, a Japanese advance against Kunming, into Thailand except as previously indicated, or an attack on Russia, would not justify intervention by the United States against Japan.

(e) All possible aid short of actual war against Japan should be extended to the Chinese Central Government.

(f) In case it is decided to undertake war against Japan, complete coordinated action in the diplomatic, economic, and military fields, should be undertaken in common by the

United States, the British Commonwealth, and the Netherlands East Indies.

The Chief of Naval Operations and the Chief of Staff recommend that the United States policy in the Far East be based on the above conclusions.

Specifically, they recommend:

That the dispatch of United States armed forces for intervention against Japan in China be disapproved.

That material aid to China be accelerated consonant with the needs of Russia, Great Britain, and our own forces.

That aid to the American Volunteer Group [the Flying Tigers] be continued and accelerated to the maximum practicable extent.

That no ultimatum be delivered to Japan.[12]

This was good advice, and apparently Roosevelt was impressed by it. The next day, November 6, he told Stimson that he wanted to propose a six-month "truce." If, at the end of that time, the Japanese and Chinese could come to no agreement, then matters would revert to what they were before.[13]

Japan's Last Offer

On November 20, 1941, Japanese Ambassador Nomura gave to Hull the final Japanese peace proposals contained in the November 4 message from Tokyo. Japan hoped that these principles could form the basis of an agreement that would head off war:

1. Both the Governments of Japan and the United States undertake not to make any armed advancement into any of the regions in the South-eastern Asia and Southern Pacific area except the part of French Indo-China where the Japanese troops are stationed at present.

2. The Japanese Government undertakes to withdraw its troops now stationed in French Indo-China upon either the restoration of peace between Japan and China or the establishment of an equitable peace in the Pacific area.

   In the meantime the Government of Japan declares that it is prepared to remove its troops now stationed in the southern part of French Indo-China to the northern part of the said territory upon the conclusion of the present arrangement which shall later be embodied in the final agreement.

47

3. The Governments of Japan and the United States shall cooperate with a view to securing the acquisition of those goods and commodities which the two countries need in Netherlands East Indies.
4. The Governments of Japan and the United States mutually undertake to restore their commercial relations to those prevailing prior to the freezing of the assets.

   The Government of the United States shall supply Japan a required quantity of oil.
5. The Government of the United States undertakes to refrain from such measures and actions as will be prejudicial to the endeavors for the restoration of general peace between Japan and China.[14]

These proposals adequately safeguarded all American interests in the Far East and would at least have provided a firm basis for further negotiations. Only the proposal that the U.S. halt further aid to China could have been considered unreasonable. Yet when Secretary Hull got them he "subjected these points and their implications to minute study, but it required very little scrutiny to see that they were utterly unacceptable. . . . Japan's proposals were of so preposterous a character that no responsible American official could have dreamed of accepting them."[15]

Roosevelt, on the other hand, must have been impressed by the Japanese proposal, because he responded with a similar proposal of his own. In a note to Hull he wrote:

6 months
1. U.S. to resume economic relations—some oil and rice now —more later.
2. Japan to send no more troops to Indochina or Manchuria border or any place South—(Dutch, Brit. or Siam).
3. Japan to agree not to invoke tripartite pact even if U.S. gets into European war.
4. U.S. to introduce Japs to Chinese to talk things over but U.S. to take no part in their conversations later on Pacific agreements.[16]

48

The Deadline Draws Near

Two days later, on November 22, Tokyo sent the following urgent message to Nomura extending the November 25 deadline set earlier:

> It is awfully hard for us to consider changing the date we set in my #736. You should know this, however, I know you are working hard. Stick to our fixed policy and do your very best. Spare no efforts and try to bring about the solution we desire. There are reasons beyond your ability to guess why we wanted to settle Japanese-American relations by the 25th, but if within the next three or four days you can finish your conversations with the Americans; if the signing can be completed by the 29th . . . ; if the pertinent notes can be exchanged; if we can get an understanding with Great Britain and the Netherlands; and in short if everything can be finished, we have decided to wait until that date. This time we mean it, that the deadline absolutely cannot be changed. After that things are automatically going to happen. Please take this into your careful consideration and work harder than you ever have before.[17]

To Hull, at least, the importance of this message was clear: "This message extended the deadline from November 25 to 29. After that, war."[18]

On November 25 there was a meeting at the White House to discuss the situation. This entry from Henry Stimson's diary tells us what transpired:

> Then at 12 o'clock we (viz., General Marshall and I) went to the White House, where we were until nearly half past one. At the meeting were Hull, Knox, Marshall, Stark, and myself. There the President . . . brought up entirely the relations with the Japanese. He brought up the event that we were likely to be attacked perhaps (as soon as) next Monday, for the Japanese are notorious for making an attack without warning, and the question was what we should do. The question was how we should maneuver them into the position of firing the first shot without allowing too much danger to ourselves. It was a difficult proposition.[19]

Stimson later elaborated on precisely what he meant when he spoke of "firing the first shot":

One problem troubled us very much. If you know that your enemy is going to strike you, it is not usually wise to wait until he gets the jump on you by taking the initiative. In spite of the risk involved, however, in letting the Japanese fire the first shot, we realized that in order to have the full support of the American people it was desirable to make sure that the Japanese be the ones to do this so that there should remain no doubt in anyone's mind as to who were the aggressors.[20]

In spite of this, the *modus vivendi* drafted by Roosevelt on November 20 was apparently still alive as late as the twenty-fifth, according to Stimson.[21] Yet the next day Hull decided to "kick the whole thing over" and offer no proposal at all.[22] Instead, he gave the Japanese an ultimatum that they were guaranteed not to accept since, among other things, it required a total Japanese withdrawal from China.[23] This was a fateful decision; there is strong evidence to suggest that the Japanese would have accepted a *modus vivendi* based on Roosevelt's proposals.[24]

On November 27 Stimson called Hull to find out what had happened to the *modus vivendi,* which Stimson had previously noted "safeguarded all our interests."[25] Hull told him that he broke the matter off and said, "I have washed my hands of it and it is now in the hands of you and Knox—the Army and the Navy."[26] That same day the following war warning was sent to Lt. Gen. Walter C. Short, commander of the Hawaiian Department, at Fort Shafter, Hawaii:

Negotiations with Japan appear to be terminated to all practical purposes with only the barest possibilities that the Japanese Government might come back and offer to continue. Japanese future action unpredictable but hostile action possible at any moment. If hostilities cannot, repeat cannot, be avoided, the United States desires that Japan commit the first overt act. This policy should not, repeat not, be construed as restricting you to a course of action that might jeopardize your defense. Prior to hostile Japanese action you are directed to undertake such reconnaissance and other measures as you deem necessary but these measures should be carried out so as not, repeat not, to alarm civil population or disclose intent. Report measures taken. Should hostilities occur you will carry out the tasks assigned in Rainbow Five so far as they pertain to Japan. Limit dissemination of this highly secret information to minimum essential officers.[27]

Interestingly, the British almost immediately received word of the American decision to break off talks with the Japanese and gear up for war. On November 26 Col. James Roosevelt, the president's son, went to New York to meet with William Stevenson, a British agent, and inform him of the Japanese situation. On the twenty-seventh Stevenson sent the following message to London:

> Japanese negotiations off. Services expect action within two weeks.

When asked by his superiors for the source of this report, Stevenson replied briefly: "The President of the U.S.A."[28]

November 27 also brought news that a Japanese fleet was moving south from Shanghai toward Thailand and Indochina.[29] This was quite a shock, because it appeared that the Japanese might attack British or Dutch territory without an attack on United States territory. If this happened, it would put the president in a very serious situation, due to the commitments to aid the British and Dutch that had already been made without the knowledge of the American people, who would have strongly resisted U.S. involvement. The commitments had been made when the ADB agreements were drawn up, and were confirmed in memos by General Marshall and Admiral Stark on November 5 and November 27.[30]

Confusion About the War Warning

The same day the war warning was sent, November 27, General Short received another warning message from Gen. Sherman Miles, chief of Army G-2 (intelligence):

> Japanese negotiations have come to a practical stalemate stop Hostilities may ensue stop Subversive activities may be expected stop Inform commanding general and Chief of Staff only.
>
> MILES[31]

On the basis of the two messages received on the twenty-seventh, Short assumed that the greatest danger was from subversion and sabotage.[32] Thus he replied with the following message to Washington on November 28:

Report department alerted to prevent sabotage period Liason with Navy reurad four seven two twenty seventh.[33]

When he received another message that same day urging him to take all possible precautions to guard against sabotage, he took this to be confirmation of his actions.[34] No further warnings were received in Hawaii prior to December 7, 1941.

Subsequently, the Army Pearl Harbor Board was very critical of the War Department for not making its warnings to Short more explicit and for not clearing up the confusion about what kind of alert he ought to have implemented. A portion of its report reads:

> Information . . . as to the activities of our potential enemy and their intentions in the negotiations between the United States and Japan was in possession of the State, War and Navy Departments in November and December of 1941. . . . This information showed clearly that war was inevitable and late in November absolutely imminent. . . . The messages actually sent to Hawaii by either the Army or Navy gave only a small fraction of this information. No direction was given the Hawaiian Department based on this information except the "Do-Don't" message of November 27, 1941. It would have been possible to have safely sent information, ample for the purposes of orienting the commanders in Hawaii, or positive directives could have been formulated to put the Department on Alert Number 3.
>
> This was not done.[35]

Operation Z

For years Navy planners had assumed that upon the outbreak of war with Japan, the Japanese would strike at the Pacific Fleet wherever it was located.[36] Navy planners also knew that Pearl Harbor was vulnerable to a surprise attack by aircraft carriers, a fact that had been demonstrated as early as 1932 in the Navy's annual maneuvers.[37] Despite this, in 1940 the Pacific Fleet was moved by presidential order from its permanent base in San Diego to Pearl Harbor to put pressure on the Japanese. It appears that the Japanese began planning their attack on Pearl almost immediately thereafter, and by early 1941 their plans for Operation Z were well under way.[38] Almost as soon as these plans were hatched, rumors about them began circulating in Tokyo's diplomatic community. On January 27, 1941, Ambassador Grew sent the following dispatch to Washington:

> My Peruvian Colleague told a member of my staff that he had heard from many sources including a Japanese source that the Japanese military forces planned, in the event of trouble with the United States, to attempt a surprise mass attack on Pearl Harbor using all of their military facilities. He added that although the project seemed fantastic the fact that he had heard it from many sources prompted him to pass on the information.[39]

Apparently this message was not taken seriously in Washington, and Admiral Kimmel was not added to the list of Magic-intercept recipients. He was aware, however, that highly secret information of this type was available in Washington. Soon after taking command of the Pacific Fleet Kimmel wrote to Stark requesting the information pertinent to his command:

> I have recently been told by an officer fresh from Washington that ONI [Office of Naval Intelligence] considers it the function of Operations to furnish the Commander-in-Chief [Kimmel] with information of a secret nature. I have also heard that Operations considers the responsibility for furnishing the same type of information to be that of ONI. I do not know that we have missed anything, but if there is any doubt as to whose responsibility it is to keep the Commander-in-Chief fully informed with pertinent reports on subjects that should be of interest to the fleet, will you kindly fix that responsibility so that there will be no misunderstandings?[40]

Kimmel's letter highlights the fact that there was indeed a distinct lack of communication between the three divisions of the Navy Department with responsibility for Magic: Communications, Intelligence, and War Plans. Furthermore, communications between the Army and the Navy on this subject were almost nonexistent.[41] Nevertheless, Kimmel was assured by Chief of Naval Operations Stark that "ONI is fully aware of its responsibility in keeping you adequately informed concerning foreign nations, activities of these nations and disloyal elements within the United States."[42]

The Bomb-Plot Message

The Japanese consulate in Honolulu did not use the Purple Code (which is why Kimmel was not given a Purple Code machine). Instead, it generally used two lesser codes, J-19 and PA-K2. Both of these codes had been broken by the United States and were regularly read in Washington. But Kimmel received no information from this source either. This is especially unfortunate because what was probably the most important message the Japanese ever sent regarding an attack on Pearl Harbor was sent to the consulate in J-19. This message was later dubbed the "bomb-plot message" because it established an area-coordinate system for Pearl Harbor, presumably to guide a bombing mission. It was sent on September 24, 1941, and amplified twice before the attack, the last time on November 29, when Japanese agents in Hawaii were ordered to report on the fleet continuously, even if there were no ship movements.[43] These three messages added up to what was very nearly a dead giveaway that Pearl would be the target of a Japanese air attack.

When the bomb-plot message was intercepted in Washington, the man who translated it into English, Lt. Comdr. Alwin D. Kramer, recognized its significance and placed a "flag" on it to signal its importance to whomever read it.[44] Commander Arthur H. McCollum, chief of the Far East Section of ONI, later said he had never seen a request for information as complicated as that sent to the Honolulu consulate in the bomb-plot message,[45] further evidence that this message gave good reason to believe an attack on Pearl Harbor was highly likely.

Admiral Kimmel was never told about the bomb-plot message nor ever given any instructions or intelligence based upon it. Thus it is impossible to say exactly what he would have done had he seen it. We can, however, infer what Kimmel would have done by noting what was done when the decoded message was received in the Philippines. The following is an excerpt from a staff report made in the Philippines after reception of the bomb-plot message:

> As Pearl Harbor approached, we got many of the intercepts of that period; there was a considerable time lag, since they all came via Washington; we set up our own plant during the war and eventually cut the decoding time on all local items. We were fortunate in having a real expert in our midst, the

chief signal officer, General Spencer Akin, long associated with this very sensitive type of work. . . . We saw some of the intercepts in Manila, on a relay through special channels. . . . It was known that the Japanese Consul in Honolulu cabled Tokyo reports on general ship movements. In October his instructions were "sharpened." Tokyo called for specific instead of general reports. In November, the daily reports were on a grid-system of the inner harbor with coordinate locations of American men-of-war; this was no longer a case of diplomatic curiosity; coordinate grid is the classical method for pinpoint target designation; our battleships had suddenly become "targets." Spencer Akin was uneasy from the start. We drew our own conclusions and the Filipino-American troops took up beach positions long before the Japanese landings.[46]

As noted, the instructions from Tokyo to Honolulu were expanded in November. On the fifteenth Honolulu was told: "As relations between Japan and the United States are most critical, make your 'ships in harbor' report irregular, but at a rate of twice a week."[47] On November 29—Nomura's negotiation deadline—Tokyo directed: "We have been receiving reports from you on ship movements, but in future will you also report even when there are no movements."[48] This last message not only pinpointed Pearl Harbor as a probable target, but indicated that an attack was imminent! However, there is nothing in the record that shows that anyone in high authority in Washington knew of this or the other bomb-plot messages before the attack came.

The Code-Destruct Message

In the week before the attack, much additional information became available in Washington that not only forecast an attack but gave definite indications that the attack would come soon. Colonel Otis K. Sadtler, head of Army communications, for one, recognized this fact:

The information began to assume rather serious proportions regarding the tense and strained relations between the two countries, and the number of messages about warnings of conditions that might obtain in case of hostilities really reached a climax around the middle of November, to such an extent that we were of the opinion that there might be a declaration of war between Japan and the United States on Sunday, November 30. This, as you all know, proved to be a "dud," and on Monday, December 1, if I recall the date correctly, messages that morning began coming in from Tokyo telling the consuls to destroy their codes and to reply to Tokyo with one code word when they so complied with their directive.[49]

As Sadtler noted, in the first week of December 1941 the United States intercepted a number of messages to various Japanese diplomatic missions ordering them to destroy their code machines.[50] Historically this is a move that shortly precedes the outbreak of war. Obviously, were the order not given in time an enemy power might capture the codes intact, making them worthless. If the order were given too early, the embassies and consulates would be left without vital communications during a most critical period.

When the code-destruct message was given to President Roosevelt by his naval aide, Adm. John Beardall, they had a short discussion about its significance. "Mr. President," said Beardall, "this is a very significant dispatch." Roosevelt asked, "Well, when do you think it will happen?" "Most any time," Beardall replied. On the basis of this conversation, Beardall concluded that Roosevelt considered an attack imminent.[51]

The key part of the code-destruct message was the order for the Japanese embassy in Washington—of all the Japanese embassies in the western world—to keep one code machine intact. This could only mean that the Japanese were very interested in keeping communications with Washington open for some special reason. This was interpreted as meaning that war would come against the United States. For this reason General Miles gave orders on December 3 for the military attache in Tokyo to destroy his personal code.[52]

The Three Little Ships

With receipt of the code-destruct message, war was clearly imminent. But the question was, Where would the Japanese attack? All the reports that had so far been received indicated a strong probability that the Japanese might attack the British or Dutch without attacking the U.S. Because President Roosevelt feared having to commit the United States to war under such circumstances, as required by agreements with the British and Dutch, he formulated a new plan on December 2 and sent the following message through Admiral Stark to Adm. Thomas Hart in the Philippines:

President directs that the following be done as soon as possible and within two days if possible after receipt of this dispatch. Charter 3 small vessels to form a "defensive information patrol." Minimum requirements to establish identity as United States men-of-war are command by a naval officer and to mount a small gun and one machine gun would suffice. Filipino crews may be employed with minimum number naval ratings to accomplish purpose which is to observe and report by radio Japanese movements in west China Sea and Gulf of Siam. One vessel to be stationed between Hainan and Hue one vessel off the Indo-China Coast between Camrahn Bay and Cape St. Jacques and one vessel off Pointe de Camau. Use of Isabel authorized by president as one of the three but not other naval vessels. Report measures taken to carry out president's views. At same time inform me as to what reconnaissance measures are being regularly performed at sea by both army and navy whether by air surface vessels or submarines and your opinion as to the effectiveness of these latter measures.[53]

This was Admiral Hart's reply to the order:

My views as follows: The Jap movement down the Indo-Chinese coast is already defined but it remains to be seen whether aimed against the Maylay Peninsula, Borneo, or both. That the British can meet their commitment to guard as far as Cape Padaran and we should use what have left after guarding against descent on Luzon in watching for one on Borneo. Am recalling Isabel from current mission and sending toward Padaran. She is too short radius to accomplish much and since we have few fast ships her loss would be serious. Therefore have to recommend against carrying out Isabel's movement though it is improbable that can start any chartered craft within two days. Am searching for vessels for charter that are suitable but cannot yet estimate time required to obtain and equip with radio. Army planes are reconnoitering sector northerly from Luzon and eastward from Sanbernardino. Navy planes northwesterly from Luzon, also covering Balabac Strait and joining up with Dutch to cover Mindanao-Halmahera line, effectiveness is problematical but as great effort as available forces can sustain continuously. Two cruisers, two desdivs [destroyer divisions] are deployed well south, remainder surface forces on local or repairing.

Have five submarines out now, remainder either placed in readiness for defensive missions or held here prepared for offensive tasks. When it is considered called for will increase air patrols and send out more subs.[54]

Hart was already taking all the measures necessary to keep Washington informed as to the progress of the Japanese fleet. Since he knew that Washington was aware of this fact, he saw immediately that there was more to the order than just a call for more patrols. Of course, the very fact that it was a presidential order signaled its unique nature. Indeed, the fact that it was a presidential order was an indispensable requirement for the plan's success. Otherwise Hart may have been inclined to ignore it as superfluous. But since the order called for an obvious suicide mission, he delayed obeying it as long as possible. According to Admiral Stark, only one ship, the *Isabel,* got out of port before December 7.[55]

Actually, there was one other little vessel that was outfitted to participate in this mission. Her name was the *Lanikai* and her commander was Lt. Kemp Tolley. Many years later Tolley recalled his mission and its purpose:

> The *Isabel* was a 900-ton yacht of World War I vintage, painted white with buff stacks and upper-works. Her battery of four little three-inch guns was inconspicuous. She would provide far better bait to a trigger-happy Japanese aviator, if illuminated at night by an offshore Japanese picket destroyer, for example, than would an unmistakable warship. It is for this reason that I believe she was specified by Roosevelt, basically the same reason as in the case of the chartered schooners. After all, there were five or six minesweepers, or similar ships of no more value than the *Isabel,* which could equally well have been used.
>
> I agree . . . that without a radio, the *Lanikai* was useless as a reconnaissance ship. In my opinion, she wasn't one. And if the gentle reader thinks a 75-foot schooner, *with* a workable radio, could ever have gotten up on a hand-keyed radio telegraph circuit and screamed for help after a four-inch straddle or a hundred-pound bomb, he is either naive or no radioman.
>
> If indeed the *Lanikai* was a decoy, it would have been

up to one of our reconnaissance eyes (or communications intercepts) to report that the *Lanikai* was there yesterday, gone today, and presumed sunk—mission accomplished![56]

In other words, the *Lanikai* and the *Isabel* were set up to be inexpensive *casus bellorum* that would provide the minimum excuse for American retaliation. When one of these little ships was blown out of the water by the Japanese it would have been the overt act necessary for an American declaration of war.[57]

The Merle-Smith Message

On December 3, 1941, the day after Roosevelt's order to Hart about the three little ships had been sent, the one thing Roosevelt most feared happened. The Dutch came to the United States and asked for aid under the ADB agreement. The only information we have on this subject comes from a Lt. Robert O'Dell who attended a briefing in Melbourne, Australia, at which the Dutch authorities informed Colonel Van S. Merle-Smith, the American military attache, that they were ordering into effect Rainbow Plan A-2. Merle-Smith informed Washington of this development, but the message was held up by the Australians and did not reach Washington until after December 7.[58] It is not known through what other channels the Dutch request may have been communicated to Washington.

Meanwhile, the British were as concerned as Roosevelt about what might happen if the Japanese attacked them and did not attack the United States. On December 1 Lord Halifax, the British ambassador to the United States, had gone to see Roosevelt and ask him what the United States would do under such circumstances. Roosevelt told him "we should obviously all be together."[59] Halifax then asked if the United States would support British action. Roosevelt said that the British could certainly count on American support, though it might take a few days before it was given.[60] To Halifax this meant that the United States would give armed support to whatever action the British took against Japan. He reported this to Churchill, and on this basis the British informed the Dutch that they would assist them unconditionally in the event of attack.[61]

A few days later, on December 5, Halifax went to see Hull to discuss further the American commitment to war. This is Hull's memorandum of the meeting:

> The British Ambassador called at my apartment by his request.
> He said he had a message from [Anthony] Eden, head of the British Foreign Office, setting forth the British view that the time has now come for immediate cooperation with the Dutch East Indies by mutual understanding. This of course relates to the matter of defense against Japan.
> I expressed my appreciation.[62]

This would seem to be a reference to the Dutch request for armed support that Merle-Smith and O'Dell had learned about in Australia. Thus it would seem that the United States was committed to war regardless of whether or not the Japanese attacked American territory.

By now the British were confident enough of American intervention that they began to notify the dominions and the commanders in the field.[63] When word reached Sir Robert Brook-Popham in Singapore, he sought to inform American authorities of the American commitment. Admiral Hart received Brook-Popham's information on December 7 and quickly wired Admiral Stark for confirmation: "Learn from Singapore we have assured Britain armed support under three or four eventualities. Have received no corresponding instructions from you."[64]

On December 6 Roosevelt received a visit from Australian Ambassador Robert G. Casey to confirm the American commitment to intervene in the event of a Japanese attack. The American ambassador to England, John G. Winant, was also being pressed to confirm the commitment. On the sixth he asked Hull for clarification:

> British feel pressed for time in relation to guaranteeing support Thailand, fearing Japan might force them to invite invasion on pretext protection before British have opportunity to guarantee support but wanting to carry out President's wishes in message transmitted by [Under Secretary Sumner] Welles to Halifax.[65]

No one has ever discovered what was in that message from Welles to Halifax, but it undoubtedly had to do with the question of American support for a British invasion of Thailand to head off the Japanese. Casey was probably on the same mission, although there are no records of precisely what transpired.

One of the things that is known about the Casey meeting is that he discovered that Roosevelt planned to send a last-minute message to the Emperor of Japan.[66] Hull had earlier said that the message was merely "for the purpose of making a record."[67] As always, Roosevelt was covering his tracks in the event that the worst happened.

The Pilot Message

As noted earlier, many in the War Department, like Col. Otis Sadtler, had expected an attack on the weekend of November 29–30. When no attack took place and the code-destruct message came in on Monday, December 1, the liklihood of war coming on the following weekend became very great indeed. The Navy, at least, fully realized from past experience that the Japanese usually began operations on a weekend, and had notified its commanders of this fact.[68] For this reason the "pilot message" assumed great importance when intercepted on Saturday, December 6, 1941.

The pilot message informed the Japanese ambassadors in Washington that a long fourteen-part message would be coming in as a reply to Secretary Hull's ultimatum of November 26.[69] By late Saturday night, on the sixth, thirteen of the fourteen parts had been received and were transmitted to the president, the secretary of state, the chief of naval operations and others.[70] When Roosevelt had read the thirteen parts, he told Harry Hopkins, "This means war."[71] Then, according to the naval aide who delivered the message:

> Mr. Hopkins . . . expressed a view that since war was undoubtedly going to come at the convenience of the Japanese, it was too bad that we could not strike the first blow and prevent any sort of surprise. The President nodded and then said, in effect, "No, we can't do that. We are a democracy and a peaceful people." Then he raised his voice, and this much I remember definitely. He said, "But we have a good record." The impression that I got was that we would have to stand on that record, we could not make the first overt move. We would have to wait until it came.[72]

61

The fourteenth part of the message came in during the night of December 6–7. Another message indicated that the entire fourteen parts were to be delivered to the United States at precisely 1:00 P.M., Washington time. Captain McCollum related what happened after receipt of this final intercept:

Early Sunday morning, when I arrived to take over the duty in my office, where we had a special watch set since early November, the fourteenth part was coming in; and while Admiral [Theodore] Wilkinson and I were discussing the situation about 9 o'clock Sunday morning, or possibly earlier, nearly 8:30, with Admiral Stark, the instruction which directed the delivery of the note to the Secretary of State was brought in, shown to Admiral Stark, who immediately called the White House on the telephone, and the draft was taken over to the Secretary of State and to the White House. At the time, the possible significance of the time of delivery was pointed out to all hands. . . . We didn't know what this signified, but that if an attack were coming, it looked like the timing was such that it was timed for operations out in the Far East and possibly Hawaii at the time. We had no way of knowing, but because of the fact that the exact time for delivery of the note had been stressed to the ambassadors, we felt that there were important things which would move at that time, and that was pointed out not only to Admiral Stark, but I know it was pointed out to the Secretary of State. . . . [About 9:00 A.M.] I held a short discussion with Lieutenant Commander Kramer as to the significance of the time, and it was he who pointed out the time at Honolulu was 7:30 and in the Far East at dawn, and so on. . . . I took that in to Admiral Stark and pointed out the possible significance of the time in conjunction with the note, and it was also pointed out to other officers of the Division of Operations who were present at the time. Admiral Stark talked over the telephone, I think, with the Chief of Staff of the Army, who presently came over with Colonel [Rufus S.] Bratton. I was not there the whole time, and later on I came back in and by 10 o'clock that morning we were given to understand that a warning message had been sent to the Commander-in-Chief, Pacific Fleet, via Army channels.[73]

For some unexplained reason the warning to Hawaii was not sent until 11:52 A.M., barely an hour and a half before the first bombs began to fall on Pearl Harbor. This is despite the fact that

McCollum thought a warning had been decided upon at 10:00. This is the warning finally sent by General Marshall to General Short:

> The Japanese are presenting at one P.M. Eastern Standard time today what amounts to an ultimatum also [sic] they are under orders to destroy their Code machine immediately stop Just what significance the hour set may have we do not know but be on alert accordingly stop Inform naval authorities of this communication.[74]

Too Little Too Late

The Army Pearl Harbor Board later dubbed Marshall's last minute warning the "too-little-and-too-late message." It seems that not only did he wait until the very last minute to send an ambiguous warning, but he didn't even send it by priority channels. Instead he sent the warning by commercial telegraph, and it wasn't delivered until after the attack. Why Marshall did not use a scrambler telephone or high-power radio transmitter has never been explained.[75]

It is circumstances like this that, over the years, have fueled a conspiracy theory of the Pearl Harbor attack. In its most extreme form, President Roosevelt is personally accused of "setting up" the Pacific Fleet in order to get America into the war.[76] Such a conclusion cannot be sustained by the evidence.

A more likely explanation is that Roosevelt wanted an overt attack on American territory or property so as to make it possible for him to fulfill his obligations to the British and Dutch. The three-little-ships incident makes this conclusion inescapable. It is also clear that the president expected war on December 7, or shortly thereafter. His remark to Hopkins after receipt of the long Japanese intercept on the sixth confirms this. But nowhere is there any conclusive evidence that Roosevelt anticipated an attack on Pearl Harbor. If anywhere, an attack was expected in the Philippines. Evidence that is cited to the contrary is largely based on hindsight.

In the final analysis, any criticism of the Roosevelt foreign policy with respect to Japan must be based not upon a theory of conspiracy but one of the "imperial presidency." Roosevelt thought that war was inevitable under any circumstances and that the longer the United States waited before it became an active belligerent the higher the cost would be later on. But the American people were not convinced of this "necessity" and had to be circumvented. This was best done by provoking an attack by the Japanese that, hopefully, would not do too much harm. Thus this observation by Roosevelt sympathizer Thomas A. Bailey is quite pertinent:

> Franklin Roosevelt repeatedly deceived the American people during the period before Pearl Harbor. . . . If he was going to induce the people to move at all, he would have to trick them into acting for their best interests, or what he conceived to be their best interests. He was like the physician who must tell the patient lies for the patient's own good. . . . The country was overwhelmingly noninterventionist to the very day of Pearl Harbor, and an overt attempt to lead the people into war would have resulted in certain failure and an almost certain ousting of Roosevelt in 1940, with a consequent defeat for his ultimate aims.[77]

Perhaps the real question is, What would have happened if the United States had not entered World War II? If one truly believes that the world would have been overrun by Hitler and Tojo, then perhaps one can have sympathy for Roosevelt's situation. The best evidence suggests no such thing was possible.[78] In any case, the war gave rise to an evil that is at the very least equally dangerous to the United States—Soviet and Chinese communism. It is hard to see how we could be worse off.

4

Admiral Kimmel and the Battle for Redemption

Admiral Husband E. Kimmel was a central figure in the instigation of the congressional investigation of Pearl Harbor. As commander-in-chief of the Pacific Fleet, stationed at Pearl Harbor on December 7, 1941, he had a strong vested interest in its outcome. The Navy also had an interest in Kimmel's struggle. He was one of its own and his disgrace reflected on the entire service. Consequently, his redemption would clear it as well as Kimmel.

Kimmel took over as CINCPAC on February 1, 1941, replacing Adm. James O. Richardson. Richardson had been relieved quite suddenly in the middle of his normal tour of duty, for which he blamed President Roosevelt. As has been noted, Richardson had constantly pressed for return of the fleet to the West Coast and made a point of telling the president.[1] Kimmel, too, was concerned about the inadequacies of Pearl Harbor, but feared making the point too strongly lest he suffer Richardson's fate. Nevertheless, he continued to ask for needed patrol planes, antiaircraft guns, and greater information about Japanese intentions right down to December 7.[2]

Kimmel Fears an Attack

The possibility of a Japanese attack was always in Kimmel's mind. As early as April 3 he had been warned by Chief of Naval Operations Stark that "the question as to our entry into the war now seems to be *when,* and not *whether.* "[3] And only a week before the attack, the *Honolulu Sunday Advertiser* of November 30, 1941, ran this headline: "Japanese May Strike Over Weekend!"[4] Kimmel also received a war warning from Stark on November 27, 1941:

> This dispatch is to be considered a war warning X Negotiations with Japan looking toward stabilization of conditions in the Pacific have ceased and an aggressive move by Japan is expected within the next few days X The number and equipment of Japanese troops and the organization of naval task force indicates an amphibious expedition against either the Philippines Thai or Kra peninsula or possibly Borneo X Execute an appropriate defensive deployment preparatory to carrying out the tasks in WPL46 X Inform district and army authorities X A similar warning is being sent by War Department X Spenavo inform British X Continental districts Guam Samoa directed take appropriate measures against sabotage.[5]

One can see from this warning that Hawaii was not included as a specific potential target of the Japanese. Primary concern was with the Far East, where events indicated an attack was most likely. This was Admiral Kimmel's belief as well as that of almost every important military and political official, including the president. Given what was known about Japanese fleet activity, it was thought that Pearl Harbor was not a probable point of attack. Therefore, Kimmel considered that his duty lay in preparing the Pacific Fleet for immediate offensive action to reinforce the Asiatic Fleet under Admiral Hart in the Philippines, as specified in his standing orders in WPL46. Thus, when the Japanese struck Pearl Harbor on December 7, Kimmel was as shocked as everyone else. Besides the contrary indications in the limited information provided him by Washington, he had been under the not unreasonable impression that the Japanese were negotiating peace in Washington, and this further reduced his apprehension of an attack.[6]

The Knox Investigation

Immediately following the Japanese attack, President Roosevelt sent Secretary of the Navy Knox on a special mission to Hawaii to ascertain damage and establish responsibility for the disaster. Colonel Knox left Washington on December 9 and returned December 14. When he arrived in Hawaii, his first question to Admiral Kimmel was, "Did you receive my message on Saturday night?" Kimmel had not, and a thorough search of all records in Washington and Hawaii failed to show that any such message was ever sent.[7]

This was Kimmel's first hint that there was information available in Washington that might have prevented a surprise attack. Though he had known that material of a highly secret nature was available in Washington, Kimmel was totally unaware of what it might be. He made repeated requests for it to Stark, but was always assured that he was receiving all relevant intelligence.[8]

Knox made his inspection of the damage as quickly as possible and was able to place a report in the president's hands the night of December 14, almost immediately after landing in Washington. The report made several extremely important points about responsibility for the tragedy:

> The Japanese air attack on the Island of Oahu on December 7th was a complete surprise to both the Army and the Navy. Its initial success, which included almost all the damage done, was due to a lack of state of readiness against such an air attack, by both branches of the service. This statement was made by me to both General Short and Admiral Kimmel, and both agreed that it is entirely true. . . . Neither Short nor Kimmel, at the time of the attack, had any knowledge of the plain intimations of some surprise move, made clear in Washington, through the interception of Japanese instructions to Nomura, in which a surprise move of some kind was clearly indicated by the insistence upon the precise time of Nomura's reply to Hull, at one o'clock on Sunday. . . . Of course, the best means of defense against air attack consists of fighter planes. Lack of an adequate number of this type of aircraft available to the Army for the defense of the Island, is due to the diversion of this type before the outbreak of the war, to the British, the Chinese, the Dutch and the Russians.[9]

Upon Knox's return, Roosevelt sought to head off bickering over responsibility between the Army and Navy by ordering the secretaries of war and navy to assume equal blame at immediate press conferences.[10] Knox released a statement to the press the very next day, December 15, while Henry L. Stimson, secretary of war, waited until the seventeenth. This would appear to have been a calculated decision on Stimson's part to make the Navy get the first headlines acknowledging responsibility. By delaying his announcement, the Army got less attention. Furthermore, Stimson seems to have forced Knox to relieve Kimmel by ordering a replacement for General Short as early as December 10. In his press conference on the fifteenth, Knox had stated that no reassignments would be ordered until a complete investigation of the Pearl Harbor attack had been made. When Stimson publicly announced Short's relief on December 16, Knox was forced to take parallel action.[11]

The Roberts Investigation

On December 16, Stimson offered his suggestions to Roosevelt for an official investigating board. He recommended Supreme Court Justice Owen Roberts to head the panel as a man who "would command the confidence of the whole country." He also suggested that Generals Frank McCoy and Joseph T. McNarney be representatives of the War Department. Stimson emphasized that he and General Marshall, army chief of staff, were "united on all the foregoing suggestions."[12] As a result, Roberts was named by Roosevelt to head a commission to investigate Pearl Harbor. McNarney and McCoy were also named to the panel. The Navy representatives were Admirals William H. Standley and Joseph M. Reeves.

Standley recalled that he received his orders on December 17 while on duty in San Diego. He left immediately for Washington, but was unable to arrive before the Roberts Commission had already convened.[13] The same day Standley got his orders, the commission, with only Standley absent, held its first meeting—in Secretary Stimson's office.[14] Thus it got Stimson's side of the story a full day before it was officially constituted by Roosevelt's executive order.[15]

When Standley finally arrived, the commission was in the midst of its first official meeting at the Munitions Building in Washington. The other members made room for him at the table and proceeded with the questioning of Adm. Richmond Kelly Turner, chief of naval war plans, and Admiral Stark. "I had not been seated there very long," Standley recalled, "before I realized that either McNarney ought to be sitting beside Turner as a defendant or Turner ought to be in my seat as a member. The latter alternative would have suited me much better, for, of all the difficult and onerous duties in a long career of public service, my membership on that Presidential Commission was beyond comparison the most unpleasant."[16]

Standley was upset at the highly irregular way in which the Roberts Commission had been made up, mixing civilian, naval, and military members together. He particularly could not understand why McNarney was on the commission. As a member of the Army General Staff, he could not have an objective view of the responsibilities in Washington. Indeed, Standley could not entirely hide his own prejudices:

> I knew from first-hand experience the shortcomings of our base at Pearl Harbor, for which Short and Kimmel were in no way responsible. From the beginning of our investigation, I held a firm belief that the real responsibility for the disaster at Pearl Harbor was lodged thousands of miles from the territory of Hawaii.[17]

As a result of Standley's protests about the irregularity of the commission's procedures, a joint resolution was rushed through Congress giving it the right to subpoena witnesses and administer oaths.[18] This was not done until January 3, 1942, however, after the commission had already gone to Hawaii. There it first heard testimony from Admiral Kimmel and General Short.

Kimmel was very concerned about the manner in which the Roberts Commission conducted its investigation. He was not permitted to confront witnesses or to submit evidence. He was not permitted to employ counsel, though Adm. Robert A. Theobald was allowed to assist him with his papers. He was further distressed to find that he was not allowed to examine and correct his own testimony.[19] Such procedures were justified by Justice Roberts on the grounds that Kimmel was not on trial.[20]

Kimmel was also burdened by the fact that most of his staff had already put to sea. As a result, he had no one to help him prepare his testimony nor any fleet records to consult. By contrast, General Short had retained the services of his staff and was able to give a more thorough and complete report to the commission. Consequently, according to Admiral Standley, it created "a very unfavorable reaction toward Admiral Kimmel in the minds of some members of the Commission."[21]

The commission finished its work and submitted a report to the president on January 23, 1942. Its conclusions regarding Kimmel's and Short's responsibilities were summarized as follows:

> The failure of the commanding general, Hawaiian Department, and the commander-in-chief, Pacific Fleet, to confer and cooperate with respect to the meaning of the warnings received and the measures necessary to comply with the orders given them under date of November 27, 1941, resulted largely from a sense of security due to the opinion prevalent in diplomatic, military, and naval circles, and in the public press, that any immediate attack by Japan would be in the Far East. The existence of such a view, however prevalent, did not relieve the commanders of the responsibility for the security of the Pacific Fleet and our most important outpost.

> In the light of the warnings and directions to take appropriate action, transmitted to both commanders between November 27 and December 7, and the obligation under the system of coordination then in effect for joint cooperative action on their part, it was a dereliction of duty on the part of each of them not to consult and confer with the other respecting the meaning and intent of the warnings, and the appropriate measures of defense required by the imminence of hostilities. The attitude of each, that he was not required to inform himself of, and his lack of interest in, the measures undertaken by the other to carry out the responsibility assigned to such other under the provisions of the plans then in effect, demonstrated on the part of each a lack of appreciation of the responsibilities vested in them and inherent in their positions as commanders. . . .

> The Japanese attack was a complete surprise to the commanders, and they failed to make suitable dispositions to meet such an attack. Each failed properly to evaluate the seriousness of the situation. These errors of judgment were the effective causes for the success of the attack.[22]

After having had deleted from it all references to secret codes, the commission report was made public by the president.[23] Admiral Standley signed it, though he had serious reservations about the report's conclusions. He felt that the commission had been severely hampered by being limited to examining only Army and Navy personnel and not being allowed to examine high civilian authorities in Washington.[24] Nor was the commission allowed to examine secret Japanese code intercepts available to the United States before Pearl Harbor. Mr. Justice Roberts was aware of this material but considered it irrelevant. When questioned about this fact he replied, "I would not have bothered to read it if it had been shown to us. All I wanted to know was whether the Commanders had been advised of the criticalness of this situation."[25]

Kimmel and Short Found Derelict

In view of this, it is not surprising that the commission found Kimmel and Short derelict. Kimmel, for one, was of the opinion that the Roberts Commission was simply out to "get" him:

> The conduct of the commission's investigation was without precedent. It was conducted without regard to rules, law or justice. Scapegoats had to be provided to save the administration. Apparently Short and I were elected before the commission left Washington. . . . Without affording me the opportunity to defend myself, the Roberts Commission convicted me without trial on secret evidence withheld from me and the public and published the findings to the world.[26]

Interestingly, the Roberts Commission sought in advance to make sure that its conclusions would be acceptable by directing William L. Langer to prepare a report on editorial opinions about the commission, its duties, and probable findings.[27] A key point of this report was that the public considered a congressional investigation to be unnecessary. But almost immediately after the attack there had been calls from members of Congress for a congressional inquiry.[28] In Admiral Standley's opinion, "our Presidential Commission was hurriedly ordered by the President on December 16 to forestall just such a Congressional investigation at that time."[29] The administration seems to have feared that an investigation by Congress would turn into a forum for its critics.

Secretary Stimson was quite pleased with what the Roberts Commission had accomplished. He told Justice Roberts that the report was "a masterpiece of candid and accurate statement based upon most careful study and analysis of a difficult factual situation." He was pleased with the fact that the commission had followed the lines suggested by him in his first preliminary talk.[30] Stimson further noted that "Congress and the press are showing signs of going through a ghost hunt for victims and the isolationists are beginning to take up that cry in Congress, but it seems to me that the report virtually met all such trials."[31]

When the Roberts report was finally released, at least one person, General Short, was utterly astonished at its findings:

> When I read the findings of the Roberts Commission on the morning of January 25th, 1942, I was completely dumbfounded. To be accused of dereliction of duty after almost forty years of loyal and competent service was beyond my comprehension. I immediately called General Marshall on the telephone. He was an old, trusted friend of thirty-nine years standing. He said he had been in New York and had not seen the report until that minute. I asked him what I should do, having the country and the war in mind, should I retire? He replied, "Stand pat, but if it becomes necessary I will use this conversation as authority."
>
> I told him I would place myself entirely in his hands, having faith in his judgment and loyalty. After I hung up I decided it wasn't quite fair to him to have to use the conversation as authority, so I wrote out a formal application which I enclosed in a personal letter to him.[32]

There was some concern within the administration for protecting Short and Kimmel from courts-martial held at a time when passions might prevent a fair judgment.[33] Yet it is clear that the administration had already done much to prejudice their cases through the public release of the Roberts report. It is more than a little likely that the administration was thinking more about protecting itself than protecting Short and Kimmel.

Kimmel Resigns

Kimmel received a call from Rear Adm. John W. Greenslade informing him that Short had resigned. Apparently Short's offer to retire had been accepted by Marshall as soon as he received it, though Short was not told of Marshall's decision.[34] When told of Short's action, Kimmel inferred that he too should retire. "Up to that time," he said, "I had not considered submitting any request for retirement; it never entered my head. I thought the matter over and decided if that was the way the Navy Department wanted to arrange this affair that I would not stand in their way. I wrote a request for retirement and I submitted it."[35]

Kimmel's retirement was ordered by Secretary Knox on February 16, 1942, effective March 1. Kimmel took this to mean that there was nothing left to do. Admiral Stark confirmed this opinion by telling him "there is no reason why you should not settle yourself in a quiet nook somewhere and let Old Father Time help this entire situation, which I feel he will—if for no other reason than that he always has."[36] In truth, there was little else Kimmel could do, so he quietly left the service to which he had devoted over forty years of his life and went to work for a private ship-building firm.

The terms of his retirement indicated that Kimmel could still be brought up for court-martial some time in the future. There is a two-year statute of limitations on such trials, however, so as the end of 1943 neared, there were calls for an extension of the statute of limitations. On December 6, 1943, Representative Dewey Short (R.-Mo.) introduced a resolution calling for such an extension. Clearly, Short's idea was to use this as a means of initiating a broader investigation that would include scrutiny of the actions of responsible civilians. In the Senate, other prewar anti-interventionists called for extension of the deadline for prosecutions. Senator Bennett Champ Clark (D.-Mo.) was of the opinion that certain individuals were "conniving" to postpone the trial of Kimmel and Short in order to protect themselves from scrutiny. The result was a compromise extension of six months.[37]

In Kimmel's case, this move was unnecessary since he had been advised by the secretary of the navy to waive the statute of limitations and had done so in September 1943. At this time Kimmel also submitted his resignation to the Frederic R. Harris Engineering Company so he could devote himself full-time to a fight for rehabilitation. Admiral Harris refused the resignation, however, and continued to carry Kimmel on his payroll for the duration of the various Pearl Harbor investigations.[38]

Kimmel Tries to Clear Himself

Kimmel then sought out someone who could act as his counsel. He was advised to contact a retired Marine colonel named Harry Leonard. Kimmel interviewed Leonard in Washington and hired him. One of Leonard's first acts was to draft a letter to the secretary of the navy for Kimmel's signature. Kimmel did not like the letter and would not sign it, but before he could notify Leonard of this, Drew Pearson published it in his newspaper column. Kimmel wrote to Leonard asking how Pearson had obtained the letter. Leonard replied that he had given it to Pearson himself, whereupon Kimmel fired him.[39]

Needing a new counsel, Kimmel went back to Washington to ask Navy Capt. Robert Lavender to take the job. Lavender replied, "I cannot do so because I do not know enough, but I know the man who does, Charles B. Rugg, of the Boston law firm of Ropes, Gray, Best, Coolidge and Rugg." Soon thereafter, Kimmel went to see Rugg and had a two-hour interview with him. When he concluded, after castigating the Roberts Commission "with every invective at my command," Kimmel said, "If you believe what I have told you, I would like to have you act as my counsel; if you don't believe me, I don't want you." Rugg took the case.[40]

Rugg was one of the most respected attorneys in New England and had been an assistant U.S. attorney general in the Hoover Administration. It was not until many years later that Kimmel learned why Rugg took his case. It seems that right after Lavender had called him about Kimmel, Rugg consulted with the commandant of the First Naval District to find out what kind of man Kimmel was. The commandant turned out to be none other than Rear Adm. Robert A. Theobald, who had been commander of destroyers at Pearl Harbor and had acted as Kimmel's aide before the Roberts Commission.[41] Needless to say, Theobald gave Kimmel the highest possible endorsement.

The Hart Investigation

Through Rugg's actions, Kimmel induced the Navy Department to conduct a supplemental investigation of Pearl Harbor early in 1944. The investigation was to be conducted by Admiral Hart, who indicated to Kimmel that such an investigation would be to Kimmel's benefit. It was stipulated, however, that Kimmel and his counsel would not be permitted to participate in cross-examination of witnesses, so Kimmel refused to take part in the investigation in order to preserve his freedom of action.[42]

In February 1944, the same month Admiral Hart began his investigation, Kimmel received a visit from Capt. Laurence F. Safford that proved to have important consequences. Safford had been chief of Naval Communications Security and, as such, was the Navy's chief cryptanalyst, or codebreaker. In this position, Safford supervised the interception and deciphering of many Japanese messages before Pearl Harbor, including the Purple Code, or Magic, material.

Safford had been under the impression that Kimmel was aware of this secret material and receiving it before the Pearl Harbor attack. Consequently, Safford was unable to understand why Kimmel was so badly surprised by the Japanese. Then, in the middle of 1943, Safford began collecting material for what he believed was the impending court-martial of Admiral Kimmel:

> I realized I would be one of the important witnesses, that my memory was very vague, and I began looking around to get everything that I could to prepare a written statement which I could follow as testimony. That was the time when I studied the Roberts Report carefully for the first time and noted no reference to the "winds" message or to the message which [Capt.] McCollum had written and which I had seen and I thought had been sent.[43]

Thus Safford discovered for the first time that Kimmel had not received any information from the Japanese intercepts available in Washington. He immediately went to see Admiral Kimmel in New York and told him about Magic.[44] Soon thereafter, Safford was called as a witness before the Hart Inquiry and placed details about Magic into the record.[45]

The Naval Court of Inquiry

Under the terms of the congressional compromise, the extension of the statute of limitations was only to last six months. Consequently, the issue came up again in June 1944, in the midst of the presidential election campaign. Representative Short renewed his resolution for extension, but only for three months so that he would have the opportunity to raise the issue again before the election in November. He was joined in his effort by such anti-interventionists as Rep. Hamilton Fish (R.-N.Y.), who asked rhetorically, "What is the Administration trying to cover up? Who is the Administration trying to cover up? And why?"[46] The resolution passed, 305–35.

When the resolution reached the Senate, it was decided to make it another six-month extension, which was agreed to by the House in committee. The final resolution also carried a provision directing the secretaries of war and navy to conduct additional inquiries into the Pearl Harbor disaster. Both secretaries urged a presidential veto, but none was forthcoming. This resulted in establishment of the Army Pearl Harbor Board (APHB) and the Naval Court of Inquiry (NCI) in the summer of 1944.[47]

When Kimmel arrived in Washington for the NCI, he went to see Adm. Ernest J. King, chief of naval operations, and asked for permission to have an aide search the secret files for material on Pearl Harbor. Secretary of the Navy Knox had just died, but King told Kimmel, "Mr. Knox promised you access to all the files in the Navy Department so I see no reason to refuse." That same afternoon Captain Lavender was sent to the secret file room where he selected more than forty documents and had them copied. Later that evening Lavender had dinner with Kimmel, Rugg, and Edward Hanifly, one of Rugg's assistants, and told them of his discoveries. He said he found the messages referred to by Captain Safford. This was good news to Kimmel, since up to that time he had only Safford's word for the existence of the secret Japanese intercepts.[48]

When the NCI opened its hearings, Kimmel moved to have these Japanese intercepts placed in evidence before the court. This request was denied by the judge advocate on orders from Secretary of the Navy James Forrestal. Kimmel insisted that these documents were vital to his defense and repeatedly urged Secretary Forrestal to allow their submission. Eventually the Navy relented and gave the messages to the NCI. This empowered the court to make the fullest possible investigation of the Pearl Harbor attack that had yet been made.

The Army Pearl Harbor Board

The APHB was not so lucky. It was prohibited from taking any testimony that even remotely related to Magic. This prohibition went so far as to force some witnesses to perjure themselves rather than discuss it. One of these was Gen. Sherman Miles, head of G-2 (Army intelligence), who later disclosed this fact in an affidavit:

Concerning the testimony I gave before the Army Pearl Harbor Board, 8 August 1944 . . . I wish to add that I avoided any statement concerning details of information and intelligence which I had received from Top Secret sources then called "Magic," or any intimation that such sources existed. The reason I so limited my testimony was because prior to my appearance before the Board, Brig. General Russell A. Osmun and then Colonel Carter W. Clarke, of G-2, War Department, transmitted to me instructions from the Chief of Staff that I was not to disclose to the Army Pearl Harbor Board any facts concerning the radio intelligence mentioned, or the existence of that form of information or intelligence in the period preceding 7 December 1941. Accordingly, I obeyed that instruction.[49]

When Admiral Kimmel was called before the APHB on August 25, 1944, he came prepared. The last question he was asked was whether he had any additional statement to make. He then told the generals about Magic and other secret materials in the War and Navy departments that indicated the Japanese would attack the United States and that had been withheld from General Short and himself.[50] This disclosure made the APHB officially aware of the Japanese intercepts for the first time. (Actually, General Marshall had previously briefed members of the board about Magic, but did not authorize them to investigate further.) After Kimmel's presentation and the revelation that the NCI was taking testimony on the subject, Marshall reversed himself. This permitted the APHB to call additional witnesses and take testimony concerning Magic.[51]

The findings of both the NCI and the APHB contradicted those of the Roberts Commission. Both panels found the respective Hawaiian commanders virtually blameless and placed heavy responsibility on the high command in Washington. The NCI, for example, concluded:

Based on Finding XVII, the Court is of the opinion that, although the attack on 7 December came as a surprise, there were good grounds for the belief on the part of high officials in the State, War, and Navy Departments, and on the part of the Army and Navy in the Hawaiian area, that hostilities would begin in the Far East rather than elsewhere, and that the same considerations which influenced the sentiment of the authorities in Washington in this respect, support the interpretation which Admiral Kimmel placed upon the "war warning message" of 27 November, to the effect that this message directed attention away from Pearl Harbor rather than toward it.

Based on Findings XVII and XIX, the Court is of the opinion that Admiral Harold R. Stark, U.S.N., Chief of Naval Operations and responsible for the operations of the Fleet, failed to display the sound judgement expected of him in that he did not transmit to Admiral Kimmel, Commander-in-Chief, Pacific Fleet, during the very critical period 26 November to 7 December, important information which he had regarding the Japanese situation. . . .[52]

Similarly, the APHB placed primary blame for the Pearl Harbor tragedy on General Marshall, rather than General Short, on these counts:

a. Failure to advise his Deputy Chiefs of Staff, Bryden, Arnold, and Moore, of the critical situation in the Pacific so that they might act intelligently for him in his absence.
b. Failure to keep General Short fully informed as to the international situation and the probable outbreak of war at any time.
c. The delay in getting to General Short the important information reaching Washington on the evening of December 6 and the morning of December 7.
d. Noting without taking action the sabotage message of Short which presumptively was on his desk on the morning of November 28, 1941.
e. His admitted lack of knowledge of the condition of readiness of the Hawaiian Command during the period of November 8 to December 7, 1941.[53]

These conclusions caused quite a stir within the War Department and the White House. Gen. Myron C. Cramer, judge advocate general of the army, was even forced to append additional conclusions of his own to the APHB report, which contradicted those above. He said, "I am of the opinion that none of the Board's conclusions as to General Marshall are justified."[54]

Stimson and Forrestal

Similarly, Secretary Stimson also refused to accept any criticism of General Marshall. This caused some difficulty with the Navy because Secretary Forrestal agreed with the charges leveled at Admiral Stark. This made parallel action between the Army and Navy impossible.[55] Forrestal noted this problem in his diary after a talk with President Harry S. Truman:

> I told him that I hoped however that any action of ours would be concurrent with a similar action by the War Department so that the Navy should not bear the full brunt, which it does now, of responsibility for the Pearl Harbor disaster. . . . I realized that there were some oblique references to General Marshall in the Army report, I felt that his record in the war and the magnitude of his accomplishments were such that he could not have a more favorable atmosphere in which to have any such criticisms made public.[56]

Because Stimson would not accept criticism of Marshall and because of the secret nature of the references to Magic they contained, it was decided not to release the APHB and NCI reports to the public. This caused Kimmel to believe the reports were being withheld simply because they were favorable to him. The secrecy bothered Kimmel even more after Forrestal's and King's critical endorsements to the NCI report were made public while the report itself continued to be withheld.[57]

Apparently, Forrestal was for complete disclosure of the reports, but feared that the Army would not go along. He knew this would make it seem that the Navy was derelict and the Army blameless. At the same time, Stimson launched additional investigations by Colonel Clarke and Maj. Henry Clausen. Their ostensible purpose was to follow unexplored leads and dig up new evidence. Their real purpose seems to have been to discredit testimony damaging to Marshall. This may be inferred from the fact that Major Clausen's list of leads to follow was supplied by General Cramer, who had dissented from the APHB report.[58] This is not to say, of course, that good information was not uncovered. For example, Clarke eventually deflated a nasty rumor about Marshall having destroyed documents.[59] Nevertheless, the net effect of the Clausen and Clarke investigations was to "acquit" the War Department of most of the charges leveled against it by the APHB.

The Hewitt Inquiry

In self-defense, Forrestal ordered Adm. Kent Hewitt to conduct an inquiry similar to those of Clausen and Clarke. Interestingly, Hewitt was not Forrestal's first choice to head up another investigation. He first asked Adm. James O. Richardson, who told him:

> I do not consider myself available because I am prejudiced. I believe Mr. Franklin Roosevelt is primarily responsible for the disaster at Pearl Harbor and Stark is most culpable. I am greatly prejudiced against Stark and against the President so I therefore disqualify myself as an impartial investigator.[60]

Kimmel was not entirely averse to the Hewitt Inquiry when he first heard about it, though he considered it mainly an effort to stall release of the NCI report.[61] When Hewitt began his investigation, he concentrated on a particular message known as the "Winds execute," allegedly received by the Navy a few days before Pearl Harbor. His report concluded that no such message was received, since Captain Safford was the only one with a clear recollection of it. Aside from this, Hewitt does not seem to have had a clear idea of exactly what Forrestal wanted from him.[62] The fact remains, however, that Hewitt's investigation mitigated many of the harsh criticisms of the NCI report. If he had not made it, when the reports of the NCI and APHB were released the Navy would have taken disproportionate blame for bungling the warnings to Hawaii. Forrestal was more interested in protecting the Navy than in covering up evidence or trying to further incriminate Kimmel.

With the conclusion of the Hewitt Inquiry in July 1945, a phase of the Pearl Harbor investigation came to an end. From then on, it was out of the hands of the Army and Navy and became a partisan political issue. Thereafter, Kimmel had to seek his redemption in the political arena.

5

John T. Flynn and Homer Ferguson: Pearl Harbor Partisans

Those with the most to gain from a further investigation of Pearl Harbor were obviously Admiral Kimmel and his counterpart, General Short. There were, however, many others with vested interests in bringing about a full-scale congressional investigation of the disaster. They came primarily from two groups: disgruntled prewar anti-interventionists seeking to prove they were right and partisan Republicans hoping to gain politically by embarrassing Roosevelt's Democratic administration. The most notable member of the former group was John T. Flynn, prominent journalist, former columnist for the *New Republic,* and chairman of the New York chapter of the America First Committee; of the latter group, Sen. Homer Ferguson (R.-Mich.) stands out.

The Roberts Commission

There had been calls for a congressional investigation of the Pearl Harbor attack almost immediately after it happened.[1] However, these demands were successfully blocked by Roosevelt's appointment of the Roberts Commission. Adm. William H. Standley, a member of the Roberts Commission, later said that it had been constituted precisely to head off a congressional inquiry, which the administration feared would become a forum for its critics.[2] If this was the administration's purpose, it was relatively successful until 1944, when several factors combined to once again make Pearl Harbor a public issue.

Although Kimmel and Short were retired soon after release of the Roberts report, both were still liable for court-martial. Neither minded this, for each believed a court-martial would clear his name. There was a statute of limitations on such trials, however, which made an extension necessary. In December 1943 a bill providing for a six-month extension passed Congress; a further six-month extension was approved in July 1944.[3]

"The Truth About Pearl Harbor"

John T. Flynn was also taking an interest in Pearl Harbor in 1944. Dropped from the *New Republic* in November 1941 for his anti-interventionist views, he subsequently became interested in Republican politics. Convinced that Pearl Harbor was a winning campaign issue if only the Republicans would use it, he went to work on an article containing all the publicly known facts about the attack. When he finished, it was too long and too controversial for any magazine, so he published it himself as a pamphlet, *The Truth About Pearl Harbor.* He printed 30,000 copies, sending them out free because there were no channels for pamphlet distribution.[4]

Working only with published material, such as the report of the Roberts Commission and Ambassador Grew's *Ten Years in Japan,* Flynn offered an astonishing indictment against the Roosevelt Administration for lying to the public about the origins of World War II. He argued that the Battle of the Atlantic, the *Greer* incident, Lend-Lease, and the occupation of Iceland all belied the assertion that the United States was at peace before Pearl Harbor. He pointed out Roosevelt's successive provocations against Japan, including the economic embargo and rejection of peace talks with Prince Konoye, culminating in the "ultimatum" of November 26, 1941. He demonstrated that the warnings sent to Kimmel and Short took no notice of any particular danger to Hawaii and that the commanders had been denied the basic necessities for their own defense: intelligence, antiaircraft guns, and patrol planes. Finally, Flynn argued that Kimmel and Short had followed their orders to the letter, but had been betrayed by their superiors in Washington into believing that no serious threat to Pearl Harbor existed. When the attack came, the administration made scapegoats of them. Flynn laid final blame for the tragedy on the commander-in-chief, President Roosevelt.[5]

Eventually, a copy of this expose reached J. Loy Maloney, managing editor of the *Chicago Tribune,* who brought it to the attention of the *Tribune's* publisher, Col. Robert McCormick. They decided to publish the pamphlet almost in full in the October 22, 1944, Sunday edition of the *Tribune,* with a circulation of over 1.4 million. It was also sent to all papers subscribing to the *Tribune* Press Service, with a combined circulation of over 14 million.[6] In its editorial comment on the Flynn article, the *Tribune* said, "not since Zola published 'J' Accuse,' his tremendous indictment of the persecution of Capt. Dreyfuss, has so overpowering an expose been made of a governing clique seeking to save itself from disgrace by damning innocent men."[7]

Thomas E. Dewey

The next step was to get New York Gov. Thomas E. Dewey, the Republican presidential candidate, to make Flynn's Pearl Harbor charges an election issue. Flynn argued that with the evidence already in hand, the controversy over the origins of World War II was bound to supercede the fierce battle over the origins of World War I. Dewey considered such a course, deciding to go ahead with it when he learned the United States had broken the Japanese secret codes before Pearl Harbor. He planned a major speech on the subject for late September 1944.[8]

General Marshall learned of Dewey's plan and resolved to head it off. He feared that any disclosure of the broken code would cause the Japanese to discontinue its use and deprive the United States of valuable intelligence. To this end, he composed a letter to Governor Dewey on September 25, which began:

> I am writing you without the knowledge of any other person except Admiral King (who concurs) because we are approaching a grave dilemma in the political reactions of Congress regarding Pearl Harbor.
> What I have to tell you below is of such highly secret nature that I feel compelled to ask you either to accept it on the basis of your not communicating its contents to any other person and returning this letter or not reading any further and returning the letter to the bearer.[9]

At this point, Dewey stopped reading. He told Col. Carter Clarke, who had delivered the letter, that he believed the message only revealed what he already knew and that he could not believe

Roosevelt was unaware of it. Clarke immediately flew back to Washington and told Marshall what had happened. The general then composed a second letter, asking only that Dewey agree not to disclose information he was not already aware of and assuring him that neither the president nor the secretary of war had any knowledge of Marshall's actions. Under these conditions, Dewey read the letter.

Marshall candidly told Dewey the plain facts about breaking the Japanese Purple Code. He revealed that this led to construction of copies of the Japanese code machine. He said that while this source provided much valuable information prior to Pearl Harbor, it gave no indication that an attack would come there. Marshall explained that the Japanese continued to use the same basic code system throughout the war and that much important intelligence was still being derived from this source. He gave as a concrete example the fact that the American victory at Midway came about partly because of intelligence developed from Japanese intercepts. Marshall concluded by asking Dewey not to reveal the broken code for the good of the war effort.[10] Dewey agreed to this request and did not make Pearl Harbor an election issue.

In truth, Roosevelt did not know about Marshall's actions at the time, but learned about them a month later after Marshall told Harry Hopkins what he had done. When Hopkins told Roosevelt, he replied, "My opponent must be pretty desperate if he is even thinking of using material like this which would be bound to react against him."[11] He expressed hearty approval for what Marshall had done. Later, when President Truman learned the story, he too approved Marshall's actions.[12]

The question of what effect a disclosure about the broken code and Roosevelt's role in Pearl Harbor might have had on the election still arises now and then. One recent study says that "a dramatic revelation that Roosevelt was reading secret Japanese messages and still was unprepared for an attack on Pearl Harbor might have had a devastating impact on the election."[13] John Chamberlain and others have argued that Dewey could have won the election with such a revelation but that his patriotism prevented him from using the material he had. More likely, the truth is closer to Roosevelt's view that any disclosure of the broken code in wartime, when intelligence was still being derived from it, would probably have produced a reaction against Dewey. There is some evidence that he realized this and that it played a part in his decision to keep quiet about what he knew. As *Human Events* put it:

> The Chamberlain story . . . was unfortunate in saying that Dewey did not make public the story from patriotic motives, and therefore lost the election through noble self-sacrifice. High Republican circles smile at this view and say that Dewey and the Republican campaign committee decided not to tell because they feared they would be discredited for revealing to the enemy a closely guarded secret—the fact that we possessed the Japanese code. Dewey was just playing safe.[14]

The Code-Secrecy Bill

With the close of the 1944 presidential campaign and Roosevelt's fourth victory, most people once again lost interest in Pearl Harbor. Then, on March 31, 1945, Admiral Kimmel noticed a small item in the *New York Herald-Tribune* while at home in Bronxville, New York. It said that Sen. Elmer Thomas (D.-Utah) had introduced a bill the day before to prohibit the publication at any time of any material that had been sent or received by the government in secret code. Kimmel immediately realized that if this bill passed it could have serious repercussions on a future investigation of Pearl Harbor. He quickly notified his lawyer, Charles Rugg, who initiated efforts to stop passage of the bill.[15] One of the first people Rugg contacted was Sen. Homer Ferguson. Rugg told him:

> The bill seems designed to preclude further investigation into the Pearl Harbor matter, and especially to forestall the publication of the reports of both Army and Navy Courts. The Secretaries in December 1944 said that these reports could not be published during the war for security reasons. With the possible end of the war approaching, the proposed legislation would substitute an edict of silence which would perpetuate the result thus achieved of concealing the truth about Pearl Harbor and of preventing the fixing of the responsibility for that catastrophe on those who were guilty.[16]

There is some evidence to suggest that Rugg himself was an object of this bill. In his endorsement to the Naval Court of Inquiry report, Admiral King complained to Secretary Forrestal that Kimmel's lawyers were in possession of secret knowledge about the broken Japanese codes. "I know of no means of keeping these lawyers from talking in public," King wrote, "except such ethical views as they may have concerning their responsibility for not doing anything that would jeopardize war operations."[17] Control of such civilians, beyond the reach of military justice, was undoubtedly a primary motivation for the Thomas Bill.

Unfortunately, Ferguson was away from the capital when the bill was reported out of committee on April 4. On April 9 it came to the floor of the Senate for a vote. By then, Ferguson had returned to Washington, but had not yet had time to mobilize opposition to the bill. In fact, at the very moment it came up for a vote, he was across the street at the Supreme Court. When Ferguson returned, he discovered to his dismay that the bill had passed by acclamation as just another war measure. Not a single voice had been raised against it, even to demand a roll-call vote. Another of Kimmel's allies, Sen. Robert Taft (R.-Oh.), was also away from the Senate at this strategic moment. There had not been time for Rugg to notify anyone else about the bill's possible consequences. Presumably, no one thought the Senate could act so quickly.[18]

Fortunately, the House was in temporary recess, which held up further action on the bill. Ferguson acted quickly to demand reconsideration before the bill was sent to the House. This had the effect of stalling the bill, but a unanimous vote was necessary to actually have it recalled. Under these circumstances, it was decided to offer an amendment to the bill that would neutralize it.

In order to drum up support for Ferguson, Kimmel went to Washington to do some lobbying on his own behalf. On April 11 he managed to get an interview with Eugene Meyer, publisher of the *Washington Post.* Kimmel pointed out to Meyer the implications of the Thomas Bill for freedom of the press and succeeded in getting him interested. The result was a scathing editorial in the next day's edition of the *Post:*

> It is regrettable to note that we can no longer depend upon the Senate to protect the Nation against executive deprivation of our liberties. The latest illustration is S. 805, which would take away from the American people that very freedom of information which we are seeking to promote in other countries. This bill was passed on Monday without exciting a ripple, either inside or outside the Senate. Only one hearing was held, and that *in camera.* At this meeting, it is understood, the members of the Senate Military Affairs Committee heard

Army and Navy spokesmen explain that the bill was merely intended to protect official information. They accepted the bill on that absurd justification. Had not Senator Ferguson discovered the bill and asked the Senate to reconsider it, calling it, rightly, sinister, we should still be in ignorance of it. . . . Under this bill the clamp is put on all manner of disclosures that, we had thought, awaited the end of the war. The history of Pearl Harbor would be kept in oblivion. . . . Freedom of information, specifically, is our immediate crusade. . . . That the Senate on Monday blacked it out in the United States was the worst blackout the Senate has sustained in memory.[19]

President Roosevelt died the day this editorial was run. This, along with the editorial opposition and some strenuous lobbying, completely took the steam out of the bill, and it was tabled. In June, before final passage, Ferguson managed to tack on an amendment exempting "any regularly constituted committee of the Senate or House" from the bill's provisions. This left the door open for a congressional investigation of the Pearl Harbor attack.[20]

President Truman

The new president, Harry S. Truman, had already expressed some ideas about Pearl Harbor in an article for *Collier's* in August 1944, which appeared while he was still a U.S. senator.[21] In this article, he contended that a major cause for the unpreparedness at Pearl Harbor was a lack of coordination between the Army and the Navy. He implied, however, that this may have been due to personal animosity between Admiral Kimmel and General Short and to interservice rivalry. Kimmel was particularly upset at this charge and quickly fired off a letter to Truman:

Your innuendo that General Short and I were not on speaking terms is not true. Your statements alleging failure to cooperate and coordinate our efforts are equally false. General Short and I, as well as our subordinates, coordinated the efforts of our commands in close, friendly, personal and official relationships.

The real story of the Pearl Harbor attack and the events preceding it has never been publicly told. This has not been my decision. For more than two and one half years I have been

anxious to have the American people know all the facts.
. . . Until I am afforded a hearing in open court, it is grossly
unjust to repeat false charges against me, when, by official
action, I have been persistently denied an opportunity to defend myself publicly.[22]

Although Truman never replied to Kimmel's letter, he later told
James Forrestal that "he was somewhat embarrassed by something
he had written or spoken about in pursuance of the Pearl Harbor
inquiry,"[23] apparently an oblique reference to the *Collier's* article.
Perhaps because of this, Truman decided that the reports of the
Army Pearl Harbor Board and the Naval Court of Inquiry ought
to be released to the public as soon as the security of the Japanese
code intercepts was no longer a problem.[24]

On August 14, 1945, the Japanese surrendered. It now became
apparent that it was almost impossible to prevent disclosures
about the broken code or to hold off a congressional investigation.
About a week later, the first public hint of the broken code appeared in *Human Events:*

Some Washington circles say that the Republican party
during the last election campaign was in possession of copies
of secret documents concerning Pearl Harbor. The Republicans finally decided not to utilize them publicly, fearing that
they would be blamed for revealing military secrets to the
Japanese. A part of this story is the Administration's attempt
to push through a bill making it a penal offense to publish
de-coded telegrams and radiograms—a move blocked by Sen.
Ferguson.[25]

"The Final Secret of Pearl Harbor"

Meanwhile, John Flynn continued to devote himself to the
study of Pearl Harbor. He prepared a new exposé based on the
secret of the Japanese code, which he called *The Final Secret of Pearl
Harbor.* * When the Japanese surrendered, Flynn rushed it into
print. Copies of the new pamphlet were ready as early as August
21. As with the first Flynn exposé, the *Chicago Tribune* agreed to
publish it in full. This it did on September 2, 1945, in its Sunday
edition. Through syndication and the news services, large portions

---

*See Appendix Three.

of the story also appeared the same day in many other newspapers, including the *New York Daily News* and the *Washington Times-Herald.* Flynn also had 160,000 copies ready for immediate sale to the public. In its editorial the next day, the *Tribune* called this "the blackest charge ever placed against an American President and his Administration."[26]

There is some evidence that the Truman Administration tried to stop publication of Flynn's pamphlet. However, when it became clear that the *Chicago Tribune* was prepared to publish it under any circumstances, the administration responded by rushing ahead with release of the APHB and NCI reports on August 29.[27] The next day, at his news conference, Truman offered his own theory to explain Pearl Harbor:

> I have read it [the Pearl Harbor reports] very carefully, and I came to the conclusion that the whole thing is the result of the policy which the country itself pursued. The country was not ready for preparedness. Every time the President made an effort to get a preparedness program through Congress, it was stifled. Whenever the President made a statement about the necessity of preparedness, he was vilified for doing it. I think the country is as much to blame as any individual in this final situation that developed at Pearl Harbor.[28]

The Joint-Committee Investigation

This explanation satisfied no one. With Flynn's disclosures a few days later, the pressure for a congressional inquiry into Pearl Harbor became overwhelming. On Thursday, September 6, 1945, after reading of the prayer and some routine business, Sen. Alben W. Barkley (D.-Ky.), majority leader of the Senate, asked for unanimous consent to make a brief statement. He then proceeded to offer his own bill for a congressional investigation of Pearl Harbor and asked that the bill be sent to committee for consideration. Suddenly, Senator Ferguson jumped up and called for an immediate vote on the measure. Barkley was trapped. Had he hoped to bottle up the bill in committee, it was no longer possible to do so. Reluctantly, Barkley offered up his bill for passage. It was, however, an administration bill that provided for a Democratic majority on the investigating committee, to be made up of members from both the House and the Senate. Ferguson had also been prepared to offer a bill, which would have established an impartial panel. Some commentators noted that the change could have serious repercussions.[29]

Flynn was convinced that the administration never really wanted an investigation and only put forward its bill after his disclosures forced its hand:

> The Administration had things all set to squelch any investigation. They proposed to issue the Army and Navy reports on the same day as the news of the surrender of Japan—thus blanketing it out. If there was still any demand they favored court-martials which would be run by the Army and Navy and which they could control. The publication of my story in Washington on Sunday ruined that plan and demand for the investigation became so powerful that the administration decided to ask for it and thus shut off debate and rows.[30]

When the Joint Committee on the Investigation of the Pearl Harbor Attack became organized, Senator Barkley was named chairman, in place of Sen. David Walsh (D.-Mass.), who had expected to be selected. In view of Barkley's position as majority leader and Walsh's outspoken criticism of Roosevelt regarding Pearl Harbor, this move was widely interpreted as a cover-up measure. As the *Wall Street Journal* put it: "When Democrats in Congress ceased to oppose a Pearl Harbor investigation and took charge of it, putting the investigating committee under the chairmanship of the Senate Democratic leader, there was ground for suspicion that a whitewash was in the making."[31]

The other members of the committee were Senators Walter F. George (D.-Ga.), Scott Lucas (D.-Ill.), Homer Ferguson (R.-Mich.), and Owen Brewster (R.-Me.), and Representatives Jere Cooper (D.-Tenn.), J. Bayard Clark (D.-N.C.), John W. Murphy (D.-Pa.), Bertrand Gearhart (R.-Cal.), and Frank B. Keefe (R.-Wis.). Cooper served as vice-chairman.

Cover-up in Committee

Open hearings were scheduled to begin on November 15, 1945. The committee was immediately embroiled in a controversy over the question of access to documents. Soon after the appointment as committee counsel of William D. Mitchell, a former U.S. attorney general under President Hoover, it was discovered that President Truman had issued an executive order on August 28, 1945, that severely restricted the committee's access to coded material. At Mitchell's request, this order was modified on October 23 for the benefit of the joint committee.[32]

The committee was still not satisfied that it had sufficient access to relevant information since members of the armed forces, whose testimony would be so vital, might feel inhibited from talking freely unless they were afforded some protection from court-martial or other—"unofficial"—penalties. The president was asked to provide this protection and authorize civilian and military government employees to come forward voluntarily to the committee with any information they might have about Pearl Harbor.[33] Truman complied with this request on November 7, 1945.[34]

Truman's concession on coded material failed to dampen the controversy smoldering within the committee over alleged cover-up measures by the Democratic majority. The threatened explosion took place on the floor of the Senate on November 2 after an executive session of the joint committee. Senator Brewster took the floor and complained that individual committee members were being denied the right to search government files, a privilege granted to members of other congressional committees. This was being done, Brewster said, not by executive order, but by vote of the committee itself along party lines. Senator Ferguson joined Brewster in pointing out that the committee counsel was permitted to receive and develop evidence, but committee members could only wait for the start of open hearings.[35]

Senator Barkley now joined the debate, arguing that the committee was set up as a committee and could act only as a committee. This made it impossible for individual members to act on their own. Senator George suggested that the problem was actually that the Republicans distrusted the committee counsel and feared that he would not dig hard enough for evidence damaging to the Democratic administration.[36]

The Minority Staff

As a matter of fact, the minority did not have much faith in Mitchell, in spite of his nominal Republicanism. Consequently, they made early provisions for obtaining their own counsel. Unfortunately, there was no provision for a minority counsel in the bill that set up the committee. This problem was solved by John Flynn, who met with the minority members of the committee on September 26. Along with Joseph Martin, the minority leader of the House, they all agreed that the majority intended to swamp the committee with documents and rush the investigation through so that nothing damaging would come out. Flynn offered to raise private money to pay for a minority research staff. This plan relieved everyone, and Senator Brewster quickly offered to provide office space for the staff.[37]

In order to funnel money for this purpose, Flynn worked out a deal with Merwin K. Hart of the National Economic Council. Hart set up an account for the Pearl Harbor staff in the name of Helen M. O'Connor. Funds were solicited from William H. Regnery ($2,000), who at one time was the financial angel of the America First Committee,[38] and Lammot DuPont ($2,500), among others. Before the committee ended its work, over $7,000 was raised.[39]

The man selected to run this minority research staff was Percy L. Greaves, a former employee of the Republican National Committee. As the open hearings began and progressed, Greaves became the center of a controversy between the Republicans and Democrats on the joint committee.

The Hearings Begin

Public hearings started on November 15, 1945, in the big Senate Caucus Room. The order of witnesses had been determined in advance by William Mitchell. This order was set in such a way that the really controversial witnesses, who might be expected to disclose details about administration duplicity on Pearl Harbor, were all scheduled toward the end.* This frustrated the Republicans terribly. Thus, when General Marshall took the stand on December 6, the seventeenth day of hearings, the minority was ready. The majority Democrats had earlier decided that because of Marshall's recently announced mission to China, the committee ought to try and get him on and off the witness stand as quickly

---

*See Appendicies One and Two.

as possible. One by one, the Democratic committee members asked him a few cursory questions and let it go at that. When Senator Ferguson's turn came, however, he spent nearly three and a half days in his interrogation.

Ferguson's actions caused a storm within the committee, but it cannot be understood unless one realizes that after World War II no living American was more highly honored and respected than General Marshall. To subject him to such intense questioning when he stood ready to leave on a mission of the greatest importance was considered horrendous. Ferguson defended his actions as absolutely necessary in view of Marshall's position as army chief of staff at the time of Pearl Harbor, and insisted that much valuable information was uncovered as a result of his queries.[40]

The Democrats counterattacked by making an issue of Percy Greaves. On December 11, while questioning Gen. Sherman Miles, Senator Lucas asked what Greaves thought to be a stupid question. Greaves chuckled softly. Apparently Lucas was prepared to make an issue out of the incident. He asked what Greaves was doing in the hearing room. Ferguson said, "He is not rendering any services for me." Whereupon Lucas replied, "Not much!" Ferguson answered that Greaves was actually working for Senator Brewster, who was away from the hearing room that day. When Brewster heard about the incident, he quickly added Greaves to his personal staff for the duration of the hearings. Years later, Senator Barkley was to maintain that because Greaves had worked for the Republican National Committee, his involvement in the hearings proved the Republicans' partisan motives.[41]

Mitchell Resigns

A further result of Ferguson's actions was the resignation of William Mitchell as committee counsel. Mitchell's chief complaint was that "it has become increasingly apparent that some members of the committee have a different view than counsel, either as to the scope of the inquiry or as to what is pertinent evidence. This has been reflected in extensive examination by some members of the committee far beyond what the legal staff anticipated."[42] Shortly after Mitchell's announcement, Senator Barkley hinted that he too might be forced to resign in order to be able to devote full time to his duties as majority leader.[43] However, a storm of protest forced Barkley to stay on, though Mitchell did leave, taking his assistant, Gerhard A. Gesell (now a well-known federal judge), with him.

The new counsel was Seth W. Richardson, a much more outspoken Republican than Mitchell had been.[44] While this change was a distinct victory for the minority, it slowed down the investigation while Richardson familiarized himself with the proceedings and the previous testimony. In order to assist him, the committee took a short recess on January 5, 1946, and did not reconvene until the fifteenth.

Thereafter, the investigation proceeded more smoothly and at a rapid pace, with hearings often running until 10:00 P.M. Finally, on February 15, a truly dramatic event took place when Navy Comdr. Lester Schulz testified.

Throughout the hearings a tremendous amount of testimony had been taken in an effort to establish just what President Roosevelt knew about the probability of a Japanese attack on December 7, 1941. This question focused on the disposition of a long Japanese message intercepted on December 6, 1941.[45] No one could say for certain whether the president had seen this message or not. It was finally discovered that Schulz had been the naval aide on duty at the White House that night. A quick search was made for him, and he was located aboard the U.S.S. *Indiana* in the Pacific. On February 12, 1946, he was called as a witness before the joint committee. The *Indiana* immediately headed to port in San Francisco, where Schulz was hustled aboard a transcontinental airplane. The plane arrived in Washington on the morning of the fifteenth; Senator Ferguson was there to meet it. In order to prevent any hasty "briefings," Ferguson insisted on accompanying Schulz to the hearing room.[46]

That same afternoon, Schulz took the stand. His testimony was nothing short of sensational. Schulz testified that he had personally taken the Japanese intercept in to Roosevelt on the night of December 6, 1941. Harry Hopkins had been the only other person present. Roosevelt read the message and handed it to Hopkins. When Hopkins handed it back to Roosevelt, in Schulz's words, "the President then turned toward Mr. Hopkins and said in substance—I am not sure of the exact words, but in substance—'This means war.' " Continuing, Schulz said,

Mr. Hopkins then expressed a view that since war was undoubtedly going to come at the convenience of the Japanese, it was too bad that we could not strike the first blow and prevent any sort of surprise. The President nodded and then said, in effect, "No, we can't do that. We are a democracy and a peaceful people." Then he raised his voice, and this much I remember definitely. He said, "But we have a good record." The impression that I got was that we would have to stand on that record, we could not make the first overt move. We would have to wait until it came.[47]

The Committee Reports

From this point on, the case against the administration was essentially complete. The hearings closed at the end of May 1946, and the members of the committee settled down to write their reports. On July 15, John Flynn received very disturbing news that Representative Gearhart, a Republican, had decided to sign the majority report. He quickly wrote a letter to Gearhart begging him not to go along with a whitewash:

I was profoundly shocked today to be told that there was some possibility of your approving the Pearl Harbor majority report. It came to me through one of my newspaper friends. I said I could not possibly conceive of your joining in a report on the Pearl Harbor disaster which both you and Scott Lucas could sign, to say nothing of Murphy. Ever since the hearings closed I have been going over this record line by line, piecing together the whole story. As we listened to the testimony, so long drawn out, so complicated, so wearisome at times, the significance was, I am sure, lost on all of us. But as I sit down to weigh all the innumerable statements of the actors who appeared before us I find the story of Pearl Harbor to be even far worse than I supposed it to be even during the hearings—worse than you supposed it to be and I know how much chagrined and shocked you were with much of it. It is only after the story is put together in this way that the enormity and culpability of the suppressions and omissions can be understood and of course nothing can prevent the full truth of this story from coming out or the role played by those who have had a part in distorting the truth and in destroying the reputations of innocent men to save the guilty ones in Washington.

For my part, I shall never stop until every man who had a hand in this business has been brought to justice.[48]

Flynn also wrote to Representative Keefe about Gearhart's defection. He must have felt very betrayed when he later learned that Keefe too had defected, signing the majority report. Keefe defended his actions on the ground that he was able to force concessions from the majority. Furthermore, he appended his own "additional views," which are, in some ways, more critical of the administration than the minority report signed by Brewster and Ferguson.[49] Flynn wrote back to Keefe:

After your statement to me over the telephone that you would never sign this report and your fear that Gearhart might do so, I was shocked beyond measure when I learned you had done precisely that. I do not believe that the "additional views" which you filed in any way cover your retreat from your own opinions in putting your signature to that report. . . . For myself, I look upon what you have done with amazement and I turn from the whole episode with a sense of disgust.[50]

Flynn subsequently took both Gearhart and Keefe to task in his newspaper column, and even years later, he continued to be bitter about their betrayal, as was historian Charles A. Beard.[51] Indeed, Flynn's worst fears were realized when liberals jumped on Keefe's and Gearhart's defections as proof that Roosevelt was innocent in the Pearl Harbor matter.[52]

With the final submission of reports, basically along party lines, and the end of formal hearings, the whole business of Pearl Harbor essentially faded away—at least in Congress. Senator Brewster voiced some comments about reopening the investigation under a Republican Congress, but Ferguson said he was not in favor of another inquiry. He said that while much important diplomatic material had been denied to the committee, another investigation could probably do no better. It was time for the historians to take over.[53]

As for Flynn, he also let the matter drop. In later years he became more concerned about Communist subversion and attached himself to Sen. Joseph McCarthy.[54] He considered writing a book about Pearl Harbor, and though he never completed it, a large manuscript can be found in his papers. As a journalist, Flynn was out of his element when not working on current events. The Pearl Harbor controversy was a matter of topical interest that confirmed his prewar beliefs and aided the short-term necessity of throwing the Democrats out of office. When that goal was reached, with the Republican victory in the 1946 congressional elections, the need for prolonging the issue was gone as far as Flynn was concerned.

6

Laurence F. Safford the Winds Execute Message

One reason why the Pearl Harbor controversy has continued to rage over the years is the complex and highly technical nature of many points raised at the hearings before the Joint Committee on the Investigation of the Pearl Harbor Attack. One of these is the mystery surrounding the so-called Winds execute message. This was undoubtedly the single most controversial issue raised throughout the entire Pearl Harbor investigation, and it all centered around one man: Capt. Laurence F. Safford.

Safford founded the Navy's communications-intelligence organization in January 1924. He continued to work in this unit on and off until 1936, when he took charge of OP-20-G, the cryptographic section of Naval Communications. In this capacity Safford participated in the massive joint Army-Navy effort to crack the Purple Code.[1]

The Winds Code

The Purple Code machines built after the code was broken enabled the U.S. government to read decrypted Japanese messages as fast as the Japanese ambassador to Washington himself. These intercepts were soon providing invaluable information not only about Japanese intentions but those of other nations as well. A standard operating procedure was soon worked out for the interception of these messages (primarily through large radio reception stations throughout the world) and their decryption, translation, evaluation, and distribution to high government officials. One of the most important of these was picked up on November 28, 1941, by Safford's branch of Naval Communications, which shared responsibility for such intercepts with a similar branch of the Army Signal Corps headed by Col. Otis K. Sadtler. This message set up the following code to be sent during Japanese-language shortwave broadcasts:

1. Japan-U.S. relations in danger: HIGASHI NO KAZE AME (East wind, rain);
2. Japan-U.S.S.R. relations [in danger]: KITA NO KAZE KUMORI (North wind, cloudy);
3. Japan-British relations [in danger]: NISHI NO KAZE HARE (West wind, clear).[2]

The appropriate signal was to be given in the middle and at the end of shortwave broadcasts, disguised as a weather forecast; each sentence was to be repeated twice. When it was heard, all secret codes and documents were to be destroyed. A similar system was set up for Japanese Morse-code broadcasts, which used the single word *higashi* for Japan-U.S. relations, *kita* for Japan-USSR relations, and *nishi* for Japan–British Empire relations.[3] Confirmations of these code systems were received from Admiral Hart in the Philippines, Consul-General Walter Foote in the Netherlands East Indies, and Col. Elliot Thorpe, senior U.S. Army intelligence officer in Java.[4]

Upon learning of this "Winds" setup, Adm. Leigh Noyes, head of Naval Communications, ordered Lt. Comdr. Alwin D. Kramer, who was the chief Japanese translator, to distribute three-by-five cards with the English translations of the code terms printed on them.[5] In the War Department, General Miles, head of G-2, instructed Col. Rufus S. Bratton, chief of G-2's Far East Section, to prepare similar cards.[6] Special measures were also taken to insure reception of Winds executes when and if they were sent. These cards allowed the person who received the intercepted message to telephone the code words picked up to the various officials involved. This was contrary to standard procedure and was intended for high-speed distribution of the information when it came in. Unfortunately, this special system meant that there would be fewer written records concerning the reception of a Winds execute than for any other Japanese intercept.[7]

Reception of the Code

Captain Safford was the first to testify about alleged reception of a Winds execute. During the investigation conducted by Admiral Hart in April 1944, he said that such an execute was broadcast during the evening of December 3, 1941 (Washington time). The combination of frequency, time of day, and radio propagation was such that the Navy picked it up only on the east coast of the United States. Safford said that Lt. Francis M. Brotherhood had been the watch officer and that the significant part of the message read "HIGASHI NO KAZE AME (East wind, rain), NISHI NO KAZE HARE (West wind, clear)," and included a negative form of "KITA NO KAZE KUMORI (North wind, cloudy)." Safford saw this message for the first time about 8:00 A.M. on Thursday, December 4, 1941, when Lt. A. A. Murray came into his office and said, "Here it is!"[8]

The next time Safford was questioned was before the Naval Court of Inquiry in the summer of 1944. This time he was unsure about whether Murray brought in the message or if Kramer did. He said the message was on yellow teletype paper and was in Japanese. Written below and underscored were the words: "War with America, War with England, and Peace with Russia." Safford was unable to locate a copy of this message, however, and implied that it had been deliberately destroyed.[9]

Safford repeated this testimony again before the Army Pearl Harbor Board, but added some new details. He said that the teletype message was about two hundred words long and that it did not conform to the system established in the message of November 28, 1941. It had words from the voice setup, but had been sent in Morse. It also used "North wind, cloudy" in a negative form, for which there was no provision in the original Winds setup.[10] Safford also admitted (1) that he did not really remember the exact words on the teletype, (2) that when Admiral Hart questioned him he had been shown a copy of the message setting up the Winds Code and from that reconstructed what he thought he had seen, and (3) that the destruction of Navy radio-station logs which would have recorded reception of the Winds execute was a matter of standard procedure whenever a receiving station moved its location.[11]

Safford testified still further before Adm. Kent Hewitt's inquiry, once again changing details. He now said that the message came in on the morning of December 4, rather than the evening of the third. He confirmed that he had no idea what reception station picked up the Winds execute, though he guessed either Cheltenham, Maryland, or Winter Harbor, Maine. He also said that Cheltenham's logs had been routinely destroyed when the station was moved to Chatham, Massachusetts.[12]

Throughout, Safford contended that the Winds execute *was* picked up, that he first saw it on the morning of December 4, 1941, and that it had been shown to him on a sheet of teletype paper. The consistent problem, however, was that other people who should have seen this intercept as well, including those named by Safford as having seen it, either could not remember doing so or flatly denied that it was ever received at all. For example, there were only four men who served as watch officers during the week of December 1–7. They were Lts. A. A. Murray, G. W. Linn, F. M. Brotherhood, and A. V. Pering. Between them, they were on duty twenty-four hours a day monitoring every message coming into OP-20-G from the various reception stations throughout the world. In turn, each one of them denied ever having seen a genuine Winds execute.[13]

Commander Kramer

Commander Kramer initially seemed to support Safford's contentions. When first questioned, before the NCI, he said: "When such a message came through, I believe either the third or fourth of December, I was shown such a message by the GY watch officer, recognized it as being of this nature, walked with him to Captain Safford's office, and Safford went directly to Admiral Noyes' office at that time." When further questioned as to what Japanese words were on the message shown to him, Kramer replied, "Higashi No Kaze Ame. I am quite certain. The literal meaning . . . is East Wind, Rain. That is plain Japanese language. The sense of that, however, meant strained relations or a break in relations, possibly even implying war with a nation to the eastward, the United States."[14]

Before the Hewitt Inquiry, Kramer began to equivocate a great deal regarding reception of the Winds execute. He still remembered seeing some kind of Winds message which he took to Safford, but no longer could recall the exact wording—of which he had previously been certain—nor to what the message referred.[15] Subsequently, before the joint committee, Kramer retreated even further from his original testimony and virtually denied having seen any kind of message at all.[16]

Safford soon began looking for explanations for this lack of support for what Safford clearly believed to have happened. He was particularly upset by the Hewitt Inquiry, which seemed to have been designed for and intent upon disproving his contentions. Safford placed primary blame on Lt. Comdr. John F. Sonnett, counsel for the inquiry. He offered the following incident as proof that Sonnett was trying to cover up reception of the Winds execute:

> I testified before Admiral Hewitt the first time on or about 24 May 1945, before he went to Pearl Harbor. I testified before Admiral Hewitt a second time on 22 June 1945, after his return from examining witnesses at Pearl Harbor. Upon completion of my testimony (in which the "Winds Execute" Message had figured), I asked him, "off the record," if there was still any doubt in his mind as to the "Winds Message" having been sent by Japan and disseminated in the War and Navy Departments. The Admiral looked startled, and before he could reply Sonnett said:
> "Of course, I am not conducting that case and I do not know what Admiral Hewitt has decided, but to me it is very doubtful that the so-called 'Winds Execute' was ever sent."
> Admiral Hewitt thought a minute or two and then said:
> "You are not entitled to my opinion, but I will answer your question. There is no evidence of a 'Winds Execute' Message beyond your unsupported testimony. I do not doubt your sincerity, but I believe that you have confused one of the other messages you were expecting to receive."[17]

Safford firmly believed that Sonnett had pulled the wool over Hewitt's eyes. Hewitt's report, taking notice of Kramer's changed testimony, the testimony of the four watch officers, that of Capt. A. H. McCollum, head of the Far East Section of the Office of Naval Intelligence, and Adm. Theodore Wilkinson, chief of ONI, who all denied ever seeing a genuine Winds execute, concluded that none had been received prior to December 7, 1941.[18]

102

Safford Investigates

In order to reconcile these discrepancies with his own clear recollection of the Winds execute, Safford began preparing extensive memoranda for himself, which later formed the basis of his testimony before the joint committee. He prepared a complex series of charts that reconstructed the Japanese news-broadcast schedules for December 3–4, 1941, with their frequencies, times, and probable reception points. This indicates that many things he later said were drawn from personal memory may actually have come from these memoranda.[19]

In his effort to prove the existence of the Winds execute and vindicate himself, Safford considered possible explanations for why the records that would prove its reception did not exist. In a memorandum to himself, he began relating a chain of circumstances beginning in January 1942, when Capt. Joseph Redman, assistant director of Naval Communications, ordered his brother, Capt. John Redman, to begin a study of Naval Communications Security. In the course of this study the latter had access to all secret files. One month later John Redman became head of OP-20-G. Safford tied this fact in with his own discovery that the Winds execute was missing from the files in November 1943 and the fact that discrete inquiries about its disappearance by Capt. E. E. Stone, who succeeded John Redman in October 1942, cleared everyone with access to the files except Redman and his assistant, Capt. Joseph Wenger. Safford drew this conclusion:

> The foregoing chain of circumstantial evidence leads to the belief that the Winds Execute Messages were removed from OP-20-G's files about 15 January 1942 on orders or at the instigation of higher authority in the Navy Department, and that the 1941 Intercept Logs for Winter Harbor and Cheltenham were destroyed at a later date to cover up this theft.[20]

He offered as further evidence Colonel Sadtler's contention that the Army's copy of the Winds execute had been destroyed on orders of General Marshall.[21] This particular myth had a long history. It got started when Sadtler told it to William F. Friedman, the Army's top cryptanalyst, who repeated it before the Hewitt and Clarke inquiries.[22] Some questioning by Colonel Clarke about this revealed that Sadtler heard this story from Gen. Isaac Spaulding. When Spaulding was called to testify, he said that he heard it from Col. John T. Bissell, who had claimed to have destroyed the documents on his own initiative.[23] Finally, Bissell testified that the whole thing was a fabrication.[24] It should be noted, however, that he probably would have said this even if he actually had destroyed some documents. Nevertheless, this incident shows how rumors and hearsay evidence combined to confuse the mystery of the Winds execute.

In another case, Safford said that Admiral Hart had told him, when he testified before Hart's inquiry, that "I have just come from the front office, and I have seen your 'Winds' message. Now, don't make statements you can't verify."[25] When the truth of this matter finally came out, Hart admitted he was mistaken and had only seen something in a history of naval communications intelligence that looked like the Winds execute.[26]

A Political Issue

Perhaps nothing further would have come of the whole Winds episode if the execute's alleged disappearance had not become a political issue in late 1945. One of the investigations conducted by the Army Pearl Harbor Board made a special point of noting in its report the "disappearance" of the Winds execute.[27] This report came into the hands of Drew Pearson, though it was still classified Top Secret, and he made it the subject of two of his newspaper columns.[28] Within a short time, the Winds execute became the topic of heated debate on the floors of the Senate and House and the object of media interest.[29]

By the time Safford testified before the Joint Congressional Committee on the Investigation of the Pearl Harbor Attack in February 1946, he knew he was the subject of much controversy. He came prepared. He opened his statement to the committee with this categorical assertion: "There was a Winds Message. It meant War—and we knew it meant War." He also said he was certain that the message was sent at 8:30 A.M. on Thursday, December 4, 1941 (Washington time), and was picked up by the Navy's radio reception station in Cheltenham, Maryland. These assertions, none of which Safford had earlier been willing to advance as being based upon his own certain knowledge, were all the result of speculation.[30]

Since the question of the Winds execute was being used as a political weapon against the Roosevelt Administration, the Democrats on the joint committee made a point of vigorously pursuing the contradictions in Safford's testimony. These were summarized in the majority report of the joint committee. It noted that circumstances which would give rise to the necessity for broadcasting the Winds execute never arose, inasmuch as international communications were not cut off prior to the Japanese attack on Pearl Harbor. On December 1, 1941, the Japanese had ordered their embassies to destroy their codes—the purpose for which the Winds execute was intended.[31] The report further noted that the Japanese denied ever sending the execute (they also falsely denied setting up the Winds system in the first place) and that the words Safford said he saw did not fit the pattern that was outlined in the setup message.[32] Furthermore, a large contingent of officials who, under normal circumstances, would have seen all intercepted messages, testified to a man that they had seen no such thing. Finally, the report said there was no evidence that the execute meant war anyway, and concluded:

> From consideration of all evidence relating to the winds code, it is concluded that no genuine message, in execution of the code and applying to the United States, was received in the War or Navy Department prior to December 7, 1941. It appears, however, that messages were received which were initially thought possibly to be in execution of the code but were determined not to be execute messages. In view of the preponderate weight of evidence to the contrary, it is believed that Captain Safford is honestly mistaken when he insists that an execute message was received prior to December 7, 1941.[33]

The "False" Execute

This raises the issue of the so-called false execute as an explanation for Safford's contentions. The history of this began with Brotherhood's testimony before the Hewitt Inquiry. He said that on the night of December 4, 1941, he received from the Federal Communications Commission what he thought was a Winds execute. He called Admiral Noyes, who said that the wind was blowing from a funny direction. It was eventually determined that the FCC had picked up a routine weather forecast.[34]

This development confuses everything considerably. Noyes often stated in his testimony before the various inquiries that he saw many false executes—that is, nongenuine "Winds" messages—and that he was the sole person to decide whether they were genuine or not. He also said that if the message described by Safford had come to him for evaluation, he definitely would *not* have considered it genuine because Safford's execute was sent in Morse but contained the voice-code words, and because the words themselves were not correct, there having been no provision for negative forms.[35] Safford, on the other hand, said he did give a message he believed to be genuine to Noyes on December 4. Noyes did not remember the incident.[36] There is, however, testimony from both Colonel Sadtler and Adm. Richmond K. Turner, head of the Navy's War Plans Division, that Noyes called them at approximately this time and discussed a Winds execute that had just been received.[37] Noyes did not recall either conversation.[38] This may have been because Noyes considered the execute nongenuine and forgot it. As Roberta Wohlstetter put it:

> In view of the confusion that occurred in 1945 in the testimony concerning the winds code on the subject of a "false Tokyo weather broadcast," it is easy to imagine this teletype being destroyed by mistake. A "false Tokyo weather broadcast" could mean either of two things: (1) an authentic execute of an authentic code that was itself a false weather broadcast or (2) a false execute of an authentic code that was a true weather broadcast. An authentic execute may have been destroyed because it was referred to as "false," and that the word was understood in the second sense, rather than in the first.[39]

In Safford's defense, therefore, he may have had a genuine execute that Noyes decided was nongenuine without telling Safford. Or the execute may in fact have been "false," although Safford continued to believe it was genuine. This would also explain why Brotherhood testified that he was still looking for a Winds execute on the evening of December 4, after the message Safford thought was genuine had come in.

Additional Evidence

The problem with all this is that if Safford's message was non-genuine, or at least considered nongenuine by Noyes, how is it that the message got passed around to higher authorities? There are several examples of testimony in which people other than Safford remembered seeing what they thought was a genuine Winds execute. Some of these have already been alluded to. For example, before the joint committee, Admiral Turner testified:

> On December 5 Admiral Noyes called me on the telephone or the interphone, I do not know which, and said "The weather message," or words to this effect, "The first weather message has come in" and I said, "Well there is something wrong about that" and he said "I think so too," and hung up.
> I never saw a draft of that, I do not know from my own knowledge where he got it from. I assumed until recently it was an authentic message.[40]

Another high Navy official, Adm. Royal E. Ingersoll, assistant chief of naval operations, also remembered seeing a genuine execute. He testified to this effect on several occasions. This is how he responded before the joint committee:

> MR. RICHARDSON. Do you recall whether your information with reference to this so-called execute came to you by reason of some writing in a dispatch or memorandum or by the telephone or orally?
>
> ADMIRAL INGERSOLL. No. I remember distinctly that officers came into my office with it. They had a piece of paper with them which purported to be a message sent in the wind code.
>
> MR. RICHARDSON. And that paper that was brought in to you, that you saw, you accepted as an execute under the wind code?
>
> ADMIRAL INGERSOLL. I understood it to be a message which had been received in the wind code.[41]

It is hard to imagine how Ingersoll could have seen this message unless it was circulated in the regular distribution system that all intercepted messages had to follow. This distribution was Commander Kramer's responsibility. It should also be remembered that in his earliest testimony Kramer unequivocally stated that he had seen a genuine Winds execute. As Roberta Wohlstetter observed: "If Kramer believed in 1941 that an authentic execute had been received, and persisted in believing so until 1945, then that is very good evidence that it was authentic."[42]

One should also note Colonel Sadtler's often stated belief that he too had been given notice of a genuine execute and that it meant war. On three different occasions he testified that Admiral Noyes called him on December 5 and said, "Sadtler, the message is in!" He then went to General Miles with the information. They were then joined by Colonel Bratton. Together they decided to get confirmation from Noyes, but were unable to do so because Noyes had left his office to report to his superiors. Perhaps Miles and Bratton decided that the lack of confirmation proved the message false. Nevertheless, Sadtler said as late as 1946 that this message made a great impression on him. "In fact," he said, "I think this is the most important message I ever received."[43] Meanwhile, Miles and Bratton both testified that no genuine execute ever came in.

Another person who swore that he saw the Winds execute was Col. Moses W. Pettigrew, who filed an affidavit with Major Clausen stating that on December 5, 1941, he had seen such an intercept from the Navy that indicated that Japanese-U.S. relations were in danger. As a direct result of this information, he was ordered to prepare the following warning for G-2 in Hawaii:

> Contact Commander Rochefort immediately thru Commandant Fourteenth Naval District regarding broadcasts from Tokyo reference weather.
>
> Miles[44]

Rochefort was the Navy's top code man in Hawaii. According to Wohlstetter, this warning "suggests that an execute may have been received on the 4th or 5th, and that since G-2 could not send any action information to the theaters, it hoped to get it to the local unit through Rochefort, who conceivably might have intercepted the same or parallel execute."[45] The joint committee majority report, however, relied on the testimony of Colonel Bratton to the effect that while no execute was picked up in Washington, it was hoped that the Navy people in Hawaii might still get it. Thus the warning did not prove reception of the Winds execute.[46] However, in light of Pettigrew's statement and the fact that Rochefort had already been ordered to look for the execute, this argument would not seem very plausible.

Another indication that the Winds execute may have been picked up, at least in the Philippines, was uncovered by Major Clausen. In Hawaii he discovered a cable from G. H. Wilkinson, a British intelligence agent in Manila, which was sent on December 3, 1941: "Our considered opinion concludes that Japan envisages early hostilities with Britain and U.S. Japan does not repeat not intend to attack Russia at present but will act in South."[47] This estimate of Japanese intentions corresponds very closely to what Safford said was in the Winds execute shown to him—war with the U.S. and Britain, peace with Russia. Thus the message may be evidence that the Winds execute was picked up by British agents in the Philippines. At least it was Major Clausen's opinion that whoever wrote this warning had the Winds execute in front of him.[48]

This incident is not as unusual as it might seem considering the history of intelligence operations in the Far East. For example, Col. Elliot Thorpe, who was head of U.S. Army G-2 in Java, obtained similar information from the Dutch, who apparently had broken some of the lower-level Japanese codes, such as PA-K2 and J-19. As previously noted, he sent confirmation of the Winds Code setup to Washington on December 3, 1941, although for some reason it did not arrive until December 5.[49] Thorpe later claimed that he also got definite information about the Japanese attack on the Philippines and Hawaii from the Dutch, though it is not clear whether this information ever reached Washington. He further states that after the war he interviewed a Radio Tokyo broadcaster who admitted sending the Winds execute. This evidence is difficult to evaluate, but it does add another dimension to the mystery.[50]

A Genuine Execute

The fact that the Japanese *did* send a genuine Winds execute *after* the attack has never been disputed, though initially the Japanese denied it.[51] For example, the FCC picked up a genuine execute on December 8, 1941.[52] Another was picked up in Hawaii on December 7, soon after the attack.[53] This latter message seems to be the same one that the Japanese admitted receiving at their consulate in Honolulu.[54] There are also other reports of genuine executes received after the attack.[55]

That a genuine execute was sent after the attack does *not* preclude the possibility that one was sent before the attack, especially in light of the reports of poor radio reception intercepted from Japanese embassies and consulates that had destroyed their codes on December 1.[56]

It was Safford's contention, moreover, that the execute sent out on the fourth was primarily intended for reception in London. The Japanese embassy there had presumably destroyed its code machine soon after the order to do so came through on the first. The embassy in Washington, on the other hand, was specifically exempted from this order.[57] Thus, according to Safford, the Japanese had no way other than the Winds Code to notify their embassy in London that war would be against Great Britain as well as the United States.[58] Support for this contention, which also takes into consideration the radio reception problems, may be drawn from the fact that on December 7 the Japanese sent the following message in plain language (uncoded) to London:

Relations between JAPAN and GREAT BRITAIN and the UNITED STATES are extremely critical.[59]

Since the wording of this message conforms rather closely to the Winds setup and because it seems to indicate some apprehension by the Japanese over reception of the Winds execute, it tends to confirm Safford's argument that the Winds execute was directed to London. No similar message was sent to Washington.

The importance of a genuine execute being picked up after the attack lies in Safford's contention that he last saw the Winds execute on December 15, 1941, when Admiral Noyes was assembling documents for the Roberts Commission. It is therefore possible he saw a "false" execute prior to December 7, but a genuine one on the fifteenth. Roberts, however, said he never saw any Winds execute, though the phrasing of some of his questions certainly implies that he knew about such a message.[60] It is still possible that Roberts was aware of a genuine execute picked up after the attack, although he also denied this.[61]

110

The Code-Destruct Orders

One last item of evidence regarding the Winds execute is Safford's statement that its reception on December 4 caused him to initiate code-destruct orders to our own naval outposts in the Pacific. These warnings carry the date of December 4, 1941.[62] Colonel Sadtler also claimed that he drafted war warnings for the commanding generals in Hawaii and the Philippines. He took them to Miles and Bratton, who dismissed the reports of receiving the Winds execute. He then went to Gen. Leonard Gerow, who thought enough warnings had already been sent, and to Col. Walter Bedel Smith, Marshall's aide, who refused to discuss it.[63] As a result, no additional warnings were sent by the Army, and the code-destruct messages sent by Safford were not explicit war warnings. Nevertheless, both Safford and Sadtler claimed that their actions resulted directly from reception of the Winds execute, and they seem to be strong evidence for its reception on December 4.

The one crucial problem left to deal with is the same one Safford himself was never able to resolve satisfactorily: What would explain the disappearance of the Winds execute and the records of its reception if it were thought to be genuine enough to reach Colonel Sadtler, Admiral Turner, and Admiral Ingersoll? Safford thought it was because the records were destroyed to hide the culpability of those who prevented adequate warnings from being sent to Pearl Harbor.[64] As evidence, he noted that one file with a number that fell between others dated December 4, 1941, was missing. This is certainly interesting, but in and of itself does not prove anything because file numbers were often skipped for one reason or another.[65]

Changed Testimony

Safford also argued that witnesses who knew about the Winds execute were harassed into changing their testimony. The key example is that of Commander Kramer, who initially supported Safford on the Winds execute and later reversed himself. Suspicion about Kramer's about-face was aroused by the fact that he testified before the joint committee that his memory on the subject was first "refreshed" after a meeting with Admiral Stark.[66] As Wohlstetter observed:

> On the whole Kramer's frequent changes in testimony are hard to understand; and one cannot help harboring some doubts about a luncheon at the home of Admiral Stark in September, 1945, where, Kramer reported, his memory was "refreshed."[67]

Why a man such as Kramer would change his sworn testimony can, perhaps, be understood when considered in light of the general reticence of military men to discuss incidents that would embarrass their superiors. Furthermore, Kramer and others knew how difficult things would be for them if they disclosed any details about the Japanese code intercepts.[68] World War II was considered a just war and Roosevelt a good president. Withholding information detrimental to either was considered the right and proper thing to do, even when a congressional committee was involved.

Safford's Actions

One last area of interest is the actions of Laurence Safford himself. He consistently maintained that the significance of the Winds execute message was that it gave three full days of warning of the Japanese attack on Pearl Harbor. As he put it in a memorandum:

> The reason for my stressing the "Winds Message" so much in my testimony (in all three cases) is because we could afford to talk about it, even print it in the newspaper, without detriment to the war effort. Even the Dutch knew of the Code and the FCC listened for the message. We had the same information—*at the same time*—from more secret but less dramatic sources. Also the "Winds Set-up" was the nearest thing to a warning CINCPAC ever got. If the "Winds Execute" had been heard at Pearl Harbor, the fleet would not have been surprised. And because CINCPAC was given no information that the "Winds Execute" had been sent, everybody at Pearl Harbor believed it had *not* been sent and that the Japs were still making up their minds as to the next step.[69]

Safford was the one man who was certain at the time that a genuine Winds execute had been received. Further, a long reply to Secretary of State Cordell Hull's ultimatum of November 26 began to come through at 1:00 P.M. on Saturday, December 6, while Safford was still on duty (the message President Roosevelt examined that evening leading him to say, "This means war."[70]). Therefore, Safford must have been the one man in the United States Navy who was sure that war would come on December 7, 1941. What, then, did he do on the evening of December 6 and the morning of December 7? He was asked about this at the time of the congressional investigation:

> MR. MURPHY. Now where were you on Saturday night the 6th of December 1941? You were asked that question before and did not answer it, but I feel this committee is entitled to an answer from you, sir. Where were you and what did you do?

> CAPTAIN SAFFORD. I was out with my wife visiting friends, and I do not recall whom we saw that morning.

> MR. MURPHY. You were still in your pajamas the next afternoon at 2:20, having breakfast, on December 7, is that right?

> CAPTAIN SAFFORD. That is right.

> MR. MURPHY. And it was the day that you expected war to start, wasn't it?

> CAPTAIN SAFFORD. Yes, sir.

> MR. MURPHY. And you are still in pajamas having breakfast at 2 o'clock?

> CAPTAIN SAFFORD. Yes, sir.[71]

This is the same man to whom the Winds execute meant "that the war would commence within two or three days in all probability, possibly Saturday, December 6, possibly Sunday, December 7."[72]

Is it reasonable, therefore, to believe that on the two days when he was sure war would come Safford would go home early, go out and visit friends, and then sleep until 2 o'clock Sunday afternoon? This point even disturbed Safford's own friends over the years, and he never gave them a straight answer. Finally, in 1967, he was forced into offering some kind of explanation for his behavior on December 6–7, 1941:

> It is the oldest trick in the book—to try to put the chief witness for the prosecution on the defensive or to try to make the victim responsible for his own murder. And that is what the cover-up crowd have done. I do not know why I said that

I stayed out late on Saturday night—if indeed I actually said it. . . . I just could not remember what I had done and it would have been better if I had said so. But remember this—Bratton changed his testimony five times. . . . I certainly have the right to repudiate and correct one piece of my testimony. Where I was Saturday night or Sunday morning was of little importance—I had no authority to do anything nor to release any warning messages. And if [General George] Marshall can rely on his wife's engagement book to "prove" where he was on Saturday evening, I have equal right to rely on my wife's memory.[73]

Where does this leave the question of whether or not the Winds execute was received? While Safford maintained throughout the entire course of the various investigations of the Pearl Harbor attack that he saw a genuine Winds execute on December 4, 1941, the limited nature of the action he took as a result casts doubt on his credibility. The fact that Safford made no effort to warn the Pacific Fleet tends to make one feel that perhaps his convictions about the authenticity of the message were not as great before Pearl Harbor as they became subsequently. It has already been pointed out that Safford was forced to reconstruct details about reception of the Winds execute from probabilities rather than personal knowledge. This was also an observation of the majority of members of the joint committee.[74] Furthermore, to be a good cryptanalyst—as Safford was—one needs to be somewhat stubborn and single-minded. In Safford's case, this meant that the more people disbelieved him, the more determined he became to prove he was right.

Of course, the testimony of other people who also claimed to have seen the Winds execute cannot be easily dismissed. Yet even Colonel Sadtler, who consistently claimed that a genuine execute was picked up before Pearl Harbor, thought it was on December 5 rather than the fourth, as Safford believed. Then again, the "false" execute may have been responsible for this discrepancy. However, there were high officials like Sadtler and Admirals Turner and Ingersoll who later stated that they too believed a genuine execute had been received—regardless of whether one really was. They—and Safford—should have acted on that belief and sent out more explicit warnings to Hawaii. This was the conclusion of the joint committee minority report and also that of historian Charles Beard.[75]

Conclusion

Unfortunately, it is still not possible to say for certain whether or not the Winds execute was really received. It is possible that a genuine message came in that was thought to be false, or that a false message came in that Safford thought to be genuine. The mixup would explain many of the contradictions in the record. Then there is also the very real question of whether or not the knowledge of a genuine Winds execute could have prepared the Hawaiian commanders for the attack. After all, Safford himself admitted that the same information was available from other sources, and the December 1 order for Japanese diplomatic missions to destroy their codes was certainly a sure tip-off of impending hostilities.

The problem all along was that virtually no one expected an attack to come at Pearl Harbor, and nothing in the Winds execute —genuine or not—specified that Pearl was a target.

The Winds issue would never have been taken so seriously if it were not for Safford's personal tenacity and if the partisan members of Congress who instigated the congressional investigation had not gone so far out of their way to prove that President Roosevelt was either absolutely guilty or absolutely innocent of allowing Pearl Harbor to be attacked. What the incident really illustrates is the extraordinarily complex nature of the Pearl Harbor controversy. Emotional questions about actions leading to the tragic deaths of thousands of men on December 7, 1941, and the role of the president of the United States in the tragedy all came down to what certain faceless men deep in the War and Navy departments thought about some intercepted Japanese messages. A small mistake in interpreting some Japanese news broadcasts was suddenly magnified a thousand times when the consequences became apparent, and it was necessary to assign responsibility. The truth of the matter will probably never be known, but the unanswered questions will still remain to be raised in similar fashion whenever powerful factions seek to determine individual responsibility for the nation's errors.

7

Isolationism and the Pearl Harbor Investigation

Following World War II, many liberals were very suspicious of those who desired a complete investigation of the Pearl Harbor attack. They feared that it would simply become a forum for debate over the origins of the war and might lead to a resurgence of isolationism similar to that which had accompanied the investigations into the origins of World War I. They were also concerned that prewar anti-interventionists still lay in wait for the opportunity to reorganize and that revisionist historians would abet a new isolationist campaign.

They were correct. Many anti-interventionists did look forward to the end of the war and the disillusionment it was sure to bring. They hoped to renew the debate over American intervention that had been suspended, but not decided, by the Japanese attack. As early as November 1942, Lawrence Dennis, a prominent isolationist and author of *The Coming American Fascism,* sought to induce the Republican Party to ride this wave of disillusionment and reestablish America's traditional foreign policy. He was certain that the liberal eastern wing of the party, which had put forward Wendell Willkie for president in 1940, was committing political suicide by echoing Roosevelt's internationalism. He expressed his ideas in a letter circulated to important prewar isolationists such as General Robert Wood of Sears:

> The only chance for the Republicans is to ride in on a post-war wave of anti-war and anti-foreign-intervention reaction. Willkie and his internationalist fellow believers want to get America into the League before the war is over, fearing that, if they don't, they can't take us in after. . . . The

idea is to take advantage of war hysteria and patriotism to bind the Republican Party to what the country does not want and seems likely to repudiate as soon as the war is over. ... If a world crusade is to be carried on, it goes without saying that the people will not take the mandate from the President who had just won the war to give it to a bright young Republican who happens to be doing a good job as governor of New York. The anti-war, anti-internationalist vote will take a walk or go to some third party candidate.[1]

The Reemergence of Isolationism

The possible reemergence of anti-interventionism became an increasing danger to Roosevelt Democrats as the end of the war came in sight. During 1944, for example, one of the president's speechwriters, Robert Sherwood, asked him if he would like to use this quotation from a recent speech by Winston Churchill: "the United States is now at the highest pinnacle of her power and fame." Roosevelt replied, "What Winston says may be true at the moment, but I'd hate to say it. Because we may be heading before long for the pinnacle of our weakness." Sherwood interpreted this to mean "that he was looking forward to the approaching moment when the reaction might set in, and isolationism again be rampant, and the American people might again tell the world to stew in its own juice."[2]

Roosevelt's successor, Harry S. Truman, was no less adamant in wishing to do all he could to prevent the resurgence of isolationism. As he put it in a letter to Sen. Harley Kilgore, "The objective of the isolationists still is to smear the Roosevelt Administration and, if possible, I am not going to let it happen."[3]

When the Joint Congressional Committee on the Investigation of the Pearl Harbor Attack went to work in the fall of 1945, the liberals' worst fears were realized. William S. White, who covered the hearings for the *New York Times,* definitely saw a revival of the prewar debate:

Memories of the bitter pre-war fight between the "isolationists" and the "interventionists" rose with an old vehemence this week as the Congressional Committee Investigating the Pearl Harbor Disaster completed its backward look into the Roosevelt foreign policy and got down to the military

117

facts of what happened and why on and before Dec. 7, 1941.

From the Republican end of the table, where the members have fallen generally into the role of cross-examiners as nearly as the Democrats seem to follow the course of sympathetic questioners, came again the suggestion, put in one way or another, that Mr. Roosevelt had been too incautiously belligerent, too "international" and too concerned with the protection of British interests in the Pacific.

On the Democratic side and while disclaimers of "politics" as such were rising from both parties, there came instant challenges, and through the room ran the recollections of speeches made in the anxious atmosphere of the Presidential campaign of 1940. The memory of Franklin D. Roosevelt was the greatest fact in the committee room.

The Republican effort was essentially to indict the policy of Mr. Roosevelt, not in its entirety but in certain phases claimed to have been significant failures. Every Republican member of the committee would have been indignant at being called "isolationist," just as every Democratic member would have protested being called "interventionist."

All this was not believed by most observers to be "politics" in the usual sense, despite whatever political profit or loss may eventually come from the hearings. What appeared to be at work was one of the deepest felt differences in American life; the cleavage between those who believed in 1939 and onward that British survival was necessary to American survival and those who believed that British survival had been at rather high cost to this country.

That this issue was profounder than politics was evident in the behavior of the spectators. They demonstrated openly for only one witness, Cordell Hull, former Secretary of State, but there were suppressed and apparently equally strong feelings for views that stood a world away from his.[4]

The Liberals Counterattack

It was not long before the liberals put up a counterattack against the isolationist undercurrent of the Pearl Harbor investigation. In the *Saturday Review,* Norman Cousins wrote, "Historians looking back at our times may find it difficult to decide what was more disgraceful—the negligence at Pearl Harbor or the conduct of the Congressional committee currently investigating the disaster."

The hearings, he continued, "have taken on some trappings of a political vendetta highly charged with vindictiveness." Cousins concluded that the committee was distorting history by making it seem that the United States was guilty and Japan innocent.[5]

The *New Republic* took this opportunity to blame its former columnist, John T. Flynn, for directing the strategy of the Republican Party on Pearl Harbor. "Quite apparently," it said, "Republican Chairman [Herbert] Brownell and other GOP high strategists were persuaded last summer that here was the great opportunity, whether or not the anti-Roosevelt charges could be proved, to weave an atmosphere of suspicion, disillusionment and distrust of the Roosevelt Administration which would harm and hamper the Democratic Party from here on in, right up to election day, 1948."[6]

A further attack on the committee came in an article for the *New York Times Magazine* by historian Allan Nevins. He stated that there was an effort being made to distort not only how America went to war, but why. Nevins blamed partisan Republicans eager to make political capital and "die-hard isolationists who seek to prove that we were betrayed into a needless war by Administration leaders who flouted the first principles of neutrality and set their own passions above the nation's welfare." He argued that this attempt, and any effort to write a revisionist history of the war, must be halted immediately or else there would be the most lamentable consequences.[7]

Even the antiadministration *Baltimore Sun* attacked the partisan effort to revive isolationism at the Pearl Harbor hearings:

> Apparently some of the Republicans have in their heads a belief that Mr. Roosevelt manipulated this country into the war with Japan as the consequence of secret commitments to Britain. Apparently some of them also have in their heads a belief that Mr. Roosevelt was responsible for some act which tipped the scales in Japan toward war. Probably such ideas derive by subconscious processes from the isolationism which affected large numbers of Republican leaders and spokesmen. They had long argued that the United States could be safe and secure if only it stayed within its borders and "minded its own business." They had seen the United States drawn into a war costly and bloody beyond calculation. In such circumstances there is a natural human tendency to seek somebody on whom can be put blame for the failure of a dogma. In the collapse of isolationism the natural tendency of many isola-

tionists was to seek an explanation, not in the facts of the world about them, but in the acts of Mr. Roosevelt and his diplomatic and military associates.[8]

The private comments of Republican leaders were also consistent in denouncing the isolationist undercurrent of the Pearl Harbor investigation. Henry L. Stimson, who had been secretary of war under Taft, secretary of state under Hoover, and secretary of war again under FDR, wrote to another old-line Republican, Thomas W. Lamont of J. P. Morgan and Company: "The attitude of the Republican leaders of the Pearl Harbor Committee is particularly stupid and unpatriotic and, so long as so many Republicans in Congress permit themselves to follow the views of the *Chicago Tribune*, they cannot expect to get very far in this international age. If they do, they will wreck the country."[9]

Unfounded Fears

The fears of a new isolationism, however, proved to be unfounded. The quickly changing world situation and the emergence of the Soviet Union as a threat prevented the United States from returning to a noninterventionist foreign policy. The Soviet threat also influenced conservatives to favor a crusade against communism. A good example of a conservative who was able to rationalize this shift is William Henry Chamberlin, a well-known journalist and expert on the Soviet Union. He argued that two developments made the anti-interventionist position untenable. First, he stated, technological changes—notably the atomic bomb and long-range aviation—meant that the United States was for the first time vulnerable to devastating attack. Second, as a result of World War II the balance of power in the world had been radically altered in favor of communism. Chamberlin argued that because of these developments the United States had to fill the power vacuums in Europe and Asia to prevent the Communists from doing so. This outlook was later popularized in such works as George Kennan's *American Diplomacy, 1900–1950*.[10]

The prewar anti-interventionists never admitted that they might have been wrong in opposing American involvement in the war. In fact, they argued that had the United States stayed out, as it should have, the Communist menace never would have arisen.

Nevertheless, they could not close their eyes to the situation as it existed after the war. As Charles Lindbergh put it in a 1945 speech, "The oceans . . . which proved effective barriers to bombing aircraft of World War II, will not protect this country from atomic rockets of World War III, if such a war begins."[11]

The Right Divided

The changing views of many prewar isolationists eventually developed into a schism between those who continued to hold to a consistent anti-interventionist position and those who allied themselves with the interventionists to resist the spread of communism. The split surfaced, for example, among the owners of the conservative weekly *Human Events*. Felix Morley, a Pulitzer Prize winner and former president of Haverford College, wanted the magazine to remain basically anti-interventionist. On the other hand, journalist Frank Hanighen and publisher Henry Regnery concluded that the threat of communism required American action abroad and thus it was no longer possible for *Human Events* to adhere to an anti-interventionist position. As a result of this clash of views, Morley parted ways with Hanighen and Regnery. To this day *Human Events* remains a leading voice of the interventionist, anti-Communist right.[12]

An odd coalition of old liberals and conservatives tried to remain true to a pure anti-interventionist policy, but found it increasingly difficult to do so. It has been argued that Senator Taft remained essentially consistent in opposing American intervention.[13] Others who also tried to do so included Lawrence Dennis, Rep. Howard Buffett, Louis Bromfield, Frank Chodorov, Garet Garrett, Oswald Garrison Villard, Charles A. Beard, John T. Flynn, and Felix Morley. Throughout the Cold War, theirs were lonely voices against interventionism, but in recent years their ideas have been rediscovered and are once again taken seriously.[14]

The Revisionists

The historical revisionists were the most hardcore adherents to anti-interventionism both before and after the war. Though they had their differences when it came to the various conspiratorial interpretations of the events leading up to Pearl Harbor, all World War II revisionists shared these basic premises: (1) nonneutrality by the United States goaded Japan into attacking Pearl Harbor, (2) intervention in Europe was not necessary to save England, and (3) the war led to the destruction of cherished American ideals. On the latter point, they followed closely the tradition of American anti-imperialism that goes back at least to 1898.[15]

The revisionist campaign began before the war was even over. In 1944, John Flynn published *The Truth About Pearl Harbor,* and in April 1945 William L. Neumann came out with *The Genesis of Pearl Harbor,* still one of the best analyses of the subject. The fall of 1945 saw the appearance of Flynn's *Final Secret of Pearl Harbor,* which precipitated the congressional investigation.

As the investigation progressed, at least two men were preparing full-scale revisionist books based upon it. The first into print was George Morgenstern, who had been commissioned by Col. Robert McCormick to write a book on Pearl Harbor while employed by the *Chicago Tribune.* With a battery of *Tribune* reporters in Washington gathering his material for him, Morgenstern was able to work very fast, publishing *Pearl Harbor: The Story of the Secret War* in 1947. Charles A. Beard, who attended many of the joint committee hearings himself, published *President Roosevelt and the Coming of the War, 1941,* a year later. The attacks heaped upon these two men for questioning accepted assumptions about the origins of the war indicated that the liberals had no intention of forgetting the pre-war debate. A particularly vicious attack on Beard, whose interpretation stands up well today as the best of the revisionist works, was launched by Samuel Eliot Morison, whose personal interest in defending the Roosevelt Administration may be shown by his position as the U.S. Navy's official historian of World War II with the honorary rank of admiral.[16]

If Beard was the best of the revisionists, the most energetic was surely Harry Elmer Barnes. A veteran World War I revisionist, Barnes was an early and outspoken opponent of interventionism, an opposition he maintained through the Korean and Vietnam conflicts. He broadened the cover-up charges made by the Republican members of the Pearl Harbor committee to include virtually the entire historical profession and the publishing industry in the United States. Barnes believed they were responsible for blocking publication of revisionist works and smearing all those that were published.[17]

Barnes' charges were not entirely ravings. Another consistent anti-interventionist historian, Richard N. Current, did indeed find that publishers did not welcome revisionist interpretations of the origins of World War II. His revisionist book, *Secretary Stimson*, had originally been submitted to Alfred A. Knopf, who, while not actually saying so, rejected the book because it was revisionist. Knopf justified this not on grounds of personal preference, but simply because he did not think such a book would sell. This was the way most publishers responded to authors submitting revisionist books. Beard did not even bother submitting *President Roosevelt and the Coming of the War, 1941*, to a commercial publisher because he believed its chances of acceptance were so poor. Instead he went directly to Yale University Press. Current followed suit and, after considerably toning down his rhetoric, had his book published by a university press also.[18]

The argument that revisionist books would not sell was never legitimate. Morgenstern's book hit the bestseller list immediately after publication, dropping off only because his publisher had not printed enough copies. By the time a second printing was ready, interest in the book had waned. Beard's book, on the other hand, went through several printings, and later revisionist books by Admiral Kimmel and Admiral Theobald not only sold very well, but were reprinted almost in toto in *U.S. News and World Report.*[19]

Revisionism and Isolationism

All these revisionist studies followed in the same path blazed by the Republican members of the Joint Congressional Committee on the Investigation of the Pearl Harbor Attack. When these men instigated the congressional investigation, they believed the path of responsibility led directly to the White House. They knew that to pursue this course it would be necessary to reopen the debate over intervention in World War II. This clearly necessitated a basically noninterventionist outlook. While there is no doubt that the Republicans believed they could make political capital out of the Pearl Harbor issue—and it probably did help them take control of Congress in 1946—they also agreed in large part with the anti-interventionist basis for the investigation.

When the hearings ended, many Republicans loudly bewailed the cover-up tactics of the Democrats and promised a new investigation when their party took control of Congress. Nothing ever came of this because it soon became clear that anti-interventionism was dead and that the investigation could not be renewed without resurrecting it, at the time an impossibility. Further contributing to the lack of congressional interest in Pearl Harbor was the depletion in the ranks of the old isolationists. Representative Hamilton Fish and Senators Gerald Nye and Bennett Champ Clark were defeated in 1944; California's Hiram Johnson died in 1945; in 1946 Senators Burton Wheeler and Henrik Shipstead were turned out of office. These key losses and the new foreign-policy bipartisanship promoted by Republican Senator Arthur Vandenberg contributed to the belief that the political wind was blowing in another direction. Consequently, even Senators Homer Ferguson and Owen Brewster, members of the Pearl Harbor committee but also good party-liners, lost interset in Pearl Harbor.

There was a general consensus that the whole Pearl Harbor business ought to be left to the historians, and that is what happened. Of the principle protagonists, Ferguson forgot the issue entirely, having been appointed to the U.S. Court of Military Appeals, where he still sits. John Flynn became more interested in anticommunism, writing books like *While You Slept* and *The Lattimore Story*. (This was not inconsistent with his anti-interventionism, however, since he continued to oppose military intervention abroad, emphasizing instead the need to stop Communist subversion at home.) In later years he worked on a book about Pearl Harbor, but died in 1964, leaving it unfinished. Admiral Kimmel maintained a life-long interest in Pearl Harbor and, together with a small cadre of fellow believers, kept alive the conspiracy theory of the attack. He died in 1968. Safford also remained interested in Pearl Harbor, but due to his wife's hatred of the subject, he was unable to pursue it. He died in 1973.

The issue of how and why the Pearl Harbor attack occurred has spawned a great literature, some writers accusing President Roosevelt personally and others blaming Kimmel or some combination of factors. Regardless of the position taken, however, the basic source of information has been and must always remain the hearings and exhibits of the Joint Committee on the Investigation of the Pearl Harbor Attack. Unfortunately, the committee documents are so large, so complicated, and so full of contradictory material, that it is almost impossible, even today, to draw a definite conclusion about many aspects of Pearl Harbor.

While it is no longer seriously believed that Roosevelt person-ally "set up" the fleet (as argued by such early revisionists as Admiral Theobald in his *Final Secret of Pearl Harbor*), one still cannot help entertaining doubts about the warnings sent to Hawaii and the intelligence denied to Kimmel and Short. Neither can one condone the way in which Kimmel and Short were treated after-ward. There is much evidence to suggest that they were chosen as scapegoats for errors that were not their own. Nor can one entirely dismiss the cover-up charges made by the Republicans and revi-sionists. The recent example of Watergate has clearly shown the extent to which men in power will try to suppress politically damaging information. There are pro and con sides to all these questions, and no existing historical evidence makes it possible to dismiss entirely either side.

Nevertheless, there are certain facts about responsibility for the Pearl Harbor attack that cannot be seriously questioned.

First, it is clear that Roosevelt wanted very badly to get the United States into the war in Europe. He believed that the only way the Nazis could be defeated was through American interven-tion, and that the Nazi tyranny was so evil that it demanded total defeat. Whether these beliefs were realistic is another question. The point is that Roosevelt and most other top government offi-cials thought so.

Second, Roosevelt was frustrated in his efforts to bring America into the war by the anti-interventionists and by Hitler's refusal to give him an incident that would justify intervention in Europe. Because of this situation, getting America involved in the war by way of conflict with Japan became the strategy. Thus, when Roosevelt began clamping down on the Japanese through em-bargoes and a refusal to negotiate in good faith, he did so with the expectation that this would eventually lead to war.

Third, during the week before Pearl Harbor Roosevelt took concrete steps to force an incident with the Japanese. This was the so-called three-little-ships strategy, which included Lieutenant Tolley and the *Lanikai,* and which is thoroughly documented.

Last, on December 6 Roosevelt expected war to come the fol-lowing day. His conversation with Hopkins leaves no doubt of this. However, it is not clear that he or anyone else in the govern-ment knew exactly where the attack would take place. Of all American territory in the Pacific, the Philippines were considered the most likely Japanese target, not Pearl Harbor. Although there

125

was evidence to suggest that Pearl might be attacked, there is nothing in the available record indicating that anyone in high authority was aware of this until it was too late.

Thus, in the final analysis, we must say that Roosevelt's guilt consisted not in a conspiracy to set up the fleet but in pursuing a policy he knew would lead to war and in failing to be honest about his intentions both before and after the attack. He should have had the political courage to say to the American people that American involvement in the war was inevitable, and the sooner the better. It is perhaps understandable why he did not do this before the 1940 presidential election, since he certainly would have been defeated, but afterward—and especially after the attack—there was no excuse for continued duplicity. And the petty effort to lay all the blame on Kimmel and Short is totally inexcusable. Further analysis may tell us more about the precise historical background of the Pearl Harbor attack, but it is not likely to diminish Roosevelt's guilt.

In any case, the most important thing about Pearl Harbor is not fixing guilt on Roosevelt or anyone else but studying the consequences. The most important of these is that Pearl Harbor destroyed American neutrality and eventually the world balance of power. Never again would it be possible to seriously advocate a purely continental policy for the United States. This is considered isolationism, the true cause of World War II according to most historians. And the destruction of Germany and Japan (not to mention England and France) created such power vacuums in Europe and Asia that American or Communist intervention became inevitable. Thus even most of those who did not blame isolationism for the war agreed such a policy was no longer viable.

It is impossible to say what would have happened if Roosevelt had not goaded the Japanese into attacking the United States. Perhaps the interventionists would have been proven correct, with Germany and Japan dominating the globe. This is highly unlikely, considering that Germany was already losing the war in the USSR by December 1941. As it turned out, the Nazis and the Japanese warlords were simply replaced by something far worse: the Communists. If the Soviet Union, with its vastly greater strength, has not yet conquered the world, chances are the Axis could not have done so either.

In spite of the vast Communist power confronting us, a non-interventionist foreign policy still might be viable. The British went to war to save Poland. Yet Poland is today enslaved. The United States intervened in Korea and fought to a stalemate. We went to war in Vietnam to save the Vietnamese from Communist domination. Yet the Communists now rule most of Southeast Asia. So, to one way of thinking, had the U.S. never intervened in World War II, Korea, and Vietnam we would now be little worse off in the international arena, and perhaps even better off (who today would deny that the Communists are a vastly greater threat to world peace than the Nazis could ever possibly have been?). In the process we would have saved thousands upon thousands of lives and billions upon billions of dollars.

Thus we must include in the final cost of the Pearl Harbor attack not only the lives of those who died on December 7, 1941, but of all those who have died since as the result of American intervention in World War II, Korea, Vietnam, and all the other engagements associated with the Cold War. This is why the origins and consequences of the Pearl Harbor attack must be understood, lest the cost of another Pearl Harbor be world destruction.

Appendix 1

Witnesses Before the Joint Committee on the Investigation of the Pearl Harbor Attack

(in order of appearance)

(1) Rear Admiral R. B. Inglis, presented Navy summary of Pearl Harbor attack.

(2) Colonel Bernard Thielen, presented Army summary of Pearl Harbor attack.

(3) Admiral James O. Richardson, former commander-in-chief, Pacific Fleet.

(4) Admiral William D. Leahy, chief of staff to President Roosevelt.

(5) Cordell Hull, secretary of state.

(6) Sumner Welles, under secretary of state.

(7) Joseph C. Grew, U.S. ambassador to Japan.

(8) General Sherman Miles, chief, Military Intelligence Service (G-2).

(9) General Leonard T. Gerow, chief, War Plans Division.

(10) General George C. Marshall, U.S. Army chief of staff.

(11) Admiral Theodore Wilkinson, chief, Office of Naval Intelligence.

(12) Admiral Richmond K. Turner, chief, War Plans Division.

(13) Admiral Harold Stark, chief of naval operations.

(14) Admiral Husband E. Kimmel, commander-in-chief, Pacific Fleet.

(15) General Walter C. Short, commanding general, Hawaiian Department.

(16) Captain Ellis M. Zacharias, USN, commanding officer, USS *Salt Lake City;* Japanese-language expert.

(17) Justice Owen J. Roberts, associate justice, U.S. Supreme Court; chairman of Roberts Commission on Pearl Harbor.
(18) Admiral William W. Smith, chief of staff to Admiral Kimmel.
(19) Captain Arthur H. McCollum, USN, chief, Far Eastern Section, Naval Intelligence.
(20) Admiral P. N. L. Bellinger, commander, Hawaiian Naval Base Air Force.
(21) Captain Laurence F. Safford, USN, chief, Radio Intelligence Unit, Office of Naval Communications.
(22) Admiral Frank E. Beatty, aide to Secretary of the Navy Frank Knox.
(23) Major John H. Dillon, USMC, aide to Secretary Knox.
(24) Captain Alwin D. Kramer, section chief and chief Japanese translator, Office of Naval Communications.
(25) Admiral Royal E. Ingersoll, assistant chief of naval operations.
(26) Lieutenant Colonel Henry C. Clausen, conducted investigation of Pearl Harbor.
(27) Colonel Rufus S. Bratton, chief, Far East Section, G-2.
(28) Colonel Otis K. Sadtler, chief, Military Branch, Army Signal Corps.
(29) Commander Lester R. Schulz, assistant to presidential aide Admiral John Beardall.
(30) Captain Joseph Rochefort, USN, communications intelligence officer, Pacific Fleet.
(31) Admiral Leigh Noyes, chief, Office of Naval Communications.
(32) Admiral Thomas Hart, commander-in-chief, Asiatic Fleet.
(33) Captain Edwin T. Layton, USN, fleet intelligence officer, Pacific Fleet.
(34) Colonel Robert E. Schukraft, chief, Radio Intercept Unit, Army Signal Corps.
(35) Colonel Walter C. Phillips, chief of staff to General Short.
(36) Lieutenant Commander John F. Sonnett, counsel to the Hewitt Inquiry.
(37) Sergeant George E. Elliot, operator at Opana radar detection station, Hawaii.
(38) Captain John M. Creighton, USN, naval observer, Singapore.
(39) Colonel George W. Bicknell, assistant chief of military intelligence, Hawaiian Department.

(40) Ensign John Phelan, counsel to Admiral Kimmel.
(41) Admiral John Beardall, aide to President Roosevelt.
(42) Captain Harold D. Krick, USN, former flag secretary to Admiral Stark.

Appendix II

Chronology of the Joint Committee on the Investigation of the Pearl Harbor Attack

1st day, Thursday, November 15, 1945, pt. 1, pp. 1–80; witnesses: Rear Adm. R. B. Inglis, Col. Bernard Thielen.

2nd day, Friday, November 16, 1945, pt. 1, pp. 81–155; witnesses: Inglis and Thielen (resumed).

3rd day, Saturday, November 17, 1945, pt. 1, pp. 157–96; witnesses: Inglis and Thielen (resumed).

4th day, Monday, November 19, 1945, pt. 1, pp. 197–266; witnesses: Inglis and Thielen (resumed), Adm. James O. Richardson.

5th day, Tuesday, November 20, 1945, pt. 1, pp. 267–313; witnesses: Richardson (resumed).

6th day, Wednesday, November 21, 1945, pt. 1, pp. 315–99; witnesses: Richardson (resumed), Adm. William Leahy.

7th day, Friday, November 23, 1945, pt. 2, pp. 401–73; witnesses: Cordell Hull, Sumner Welles.

8th day, Saturday, November 24, 1945, pt. 2, pp. 475–549; witnesses: Welles (resumed).

9th day, Monday, November 26, 1945, pt. 2, pp. 551–603; witnesses: Hull (resumed), Joseph C. Grew.

10th day, Tuesday, November 27, 1945, pt. 2, pp. 605–78; witnesses: Hull and Grew (resumed).

11th day, Wednesday, November 28, 1945, pt. 2, pp. 679–739; witnesses: Grew (resumed).

12th day, Thursday, November 29, 1945, pt. 2, pp. 741–805; witnesses: Grew (resumed), Gen. Sherman Miles.

13th day, Friday, November 30, 1945, pt. 2, pp. 807–62; witnesses: Miles (resumed).

14th day, Monday, December 3, 1945, pt. 2, pp. 863–918; witnesses: Miles (resumed).

15th day, Tuesday, December 4, 1945, pt. 2, pp. 919–82; witnesses: Miles (resumed).

16th day, Wednesday, December 5, 1945, pt. 3, pp. 983–1048; witnesses: Gen. Leonard Gerow.

17th day, Thursday, December 6, 1945, pt. 3, pp. 1049–103; witnesses: Gen. George Marshall.

18th day, Friday, December 7, 1945, pt. 3, pp. 1105–163; witnesses: Marshall (resumed).

19th day, Saturday, December 8, 1945, pt. 3, pp. 1165–234; witnesses: Marshall (resumed).

20th day, Monday, December 10, 1945, pt. 3, pp. 1235–306; witnesses: Marshall (resumed).

21st day, Tuesday, December 11, 1945, pt. 3, pp. 1307–75; witnesses: Marshall (resumed), Miles (resumed).

22nd day, Wednesday, December 12, 1945, pt. 3, pp. 1377–497; witnesses: Marshall (resumed).

23rd day, Thursday, December 13, 1945, pt. 3, pp. 1499–583; witnesses: Marshall (resumed), Miles (resumed).

24th day, Friday, December 14, 1945, pt. 4, pp. 1585–640; witnesses: Gerow (resumed).

25th day, Saturday, December 15, 1945, pt. 4, pp. 1641–717; witnesses: Gerow (resumed).

26th day, Monday, December 17, 1945, pt. 4, pp. 1719–82; witnesses: Adm. Theodore Wilkinson.

27th day, Tuesday, December 18, 1945, pt. 4, pp. 1783–858; witnesses: Wilkinson (resumed).

28th day, Wednesday, December 19, 1945, pt. 4, pp. 1859–918; witnesses: Wilkinson (resumed), Adm. Richmond K. Turner.

29th day, Thursday, December 20, 1945, pt. 4, pp. 1919–73; witnesses: Turner (resumed).

30th day, Friday, December 21, 1945, pt. 4, pp. 1975–2063; witnesses: Turner (resumed).

31st day, Monday, December 31, 1945, pt. 5, pp. 2065–146; witnesses: Adm. Harold Stark.

32nd day, Wednesday, January 2, 1946, pt. 5, pp. 2147–236; witnesses: Stark (resumed).

33rd day, Thursday, January 3, 1946, pt. 5, pp. 2237–306; witnesses: Stark (resumed).

34th day, Friday, January 4, 1946, pt. 5, pp. 2307–84; witnesses: Stark (resumed).

35th day, Saturday, January 5, 1946, pt. 5, pp. 2385–492; witnesses: Stark (resumed).

36th day, Tuesday, January 15, 1946, pt. 6, pp. 2493–554; witnesses: Adm. Husband E. Kimmel.

37th day, Wednesday, January 16, 1946, pt. 6, pp. 2555–613; witnesses: Kimmel (resumed).

38th day, Thursday, January 17, 1946, pt. 6, pp. 2615–700; witnesses: Kimmel (resumed).

39th day, Friday, January 18, 1946, pt. 6, pp. 2701–65; witnesses: Kimmel (resumed).

40th day, Saturday, January 19, 1946, pt. 6, pp. 2767–844; witnesses: Kimmel (resumed).

41st day, Monday, January 21, 1946, pt. 6, pp. 2845–920; witnesses: Kimmel (resumed).

42nd day, Tuesday, January 22, 1946, pt. 7, pp. 2921–64; witnesses: Gen. Walter C. Short.

43rd day, Wednesday, January 23, 1946, pt. 7, pp. 2965–3024; witnesses: Short (resumed).

44th day, Thursday, January 24, 1946, pt. 7, pp. 3025–90; witnesses: Short (resumed).

45th day, Friday, January 25, 1946, pt. 7, pp. 3091–160; witnesses: Short (resumed).

46th day, Saturday, January 26, 1946, pt. 7, pp. 3161–231; witnesses: Short (resumed).

47th day, Monday, January 28, 1946, pt. 7, pp. 3233–319; witnesses: Capt. Ellis M. Zacharias, Justice Owen Roberts.

48th day, Tuesday, January 29, 1946, pt. 7, pp. 3321–78; witnesses: Zacharias (resumed), Adm. William W. Smith.

49th day, Wednesday, January 30, 1946, pt. 8, pp. 3379–448; witnesses: Capt. Arthur H. McCollum.

50th day, Thursday, January 31, 1946, pt. 8, pp. 3449–519; witnesses: Adm. Patrick Bellinger.

51st day, Friday, February 1, 1946, pt. 8, pp. 3521–91; witnesses: Smith (resumed), Capt. Laurence F. Safford.

52nd day, Saturday, February 2, 1946, pt. 8, pp. 3593–671; witnesses: Safford (resumed).

53rd day, Monday, February 4, 1946, pt. 8, pp. 3673–740; witnesses: Safford (resumed).

54th day, Tuesday, February 5, 1946, pt. 8, pp. 3741–838; witnesses: Safford (resumed), Adm. Frank Beatty, Maj. John Dillon.

55th day, Wednesday, February 6, 1946, pt. 8, pp. 3839–927; witnesses: Safford (resumed), Capt. Alwin D. Kramer.

56th day, Thursday, February 7, 1946, pt. 9, pp. 3929–4007; witnesses: Kramer (resumed).

57th day, Friday, February 8, 1946, pt. 9, pp. 4009–92; witnesses: Kramer (resumed).

58th day, Saturday, February 9, 1946, pt. 9, pp. 4093–156; witnesses: Kramer (resumed).

59th day, Monday, February 11, 1946, pt. 9, pp. 4157–247; witnesses: Kramer (resumed), Adm. Royal E. Ingersoll.

60th day, Tuesday, February 12, 1946, pt. 9, pp. 4249–340; witnesses: Ingersoll (resumed), Lt. Col. Henry Clausen.

61st day, Wednesday, February 13, 1946, pt. 9, pp. 4341–460. witnesses: Clausen (resumed).

62nd day, Thursday, February 14, 1946, pt. 9, pp. 4461–599; witnesses: Clausen (resumed), Col. Rufus Bratton.

63rd day, Friday, February 15, 1946, pt. 10, pp. 4601–91; witnesses: Bratton (resumed), Col. Otis K. Sadtler, Lt. Lester Schulz, Capt. Joseph Rochefort.

64th day, Saturday, February 16, 1946, pt. 10, pp. 4693–792; witnesses: Rochefort (resumed), Adm. Leigh Noyes.

65th day, Monday, February 18, 1946, pt. 10, pp. 4793–910; witnesses: Adm. Thomas Hart, Capt. Edward Layton, Col. Robert Schukraft.

66th day, Tuesday, February 19, 1946, pt. 10, pp. 4911–5012; witnesses: Schukraft (resumed), Col. Walter Phillips, Lt. Comdr. John F. Sonnett.

67th day, Wednesday, February 20, 1946, pt. 10, pp. 5013–151; witnesses: Sonnett (resumed), Sgt. George Elliot, Capt. John Creighton, Col. George Bicknell.

68th day, Tuesday, April 9, 1946, pt. 11, pp. 5153–200; witnesses: Stark (resumed), Marshall (resumed).

69th day, Thursday, April 11, 1946, pt. 11, pp. 5201–364; witnesses: Stark (resumed), Esn. John Phelan, Adm. John Beardall.

70th day, Thursday, May 23, 1946, pt. 11, pp. 5365–542; witnesses: none.

71st day, Friday, May 31, 1946, pt. 11, pp. 5543–60; witnesses: Stark (resumed), Capt. Harold Krick.

Appendix III
"The Final Secret of Pearl Harbor"

The day after the Chicago Tribune *published the text of John T. Flynn's pamphlet* The Final Secret of Pearl Harbor—*September 3, 1945—it ran an editorial ("The Indictment") expressing indignation at what it saw as the Roosevelt Administration's negligence and culpability in the Pearl Harbor disaster and calling for further disclosure and reply to Flynn's charges. Below are reprinted that editorial and, in facsimile, Flynn's pamphlet.*

The Indictment

John T. Flynn's report on the Pearl Harbor disaster, printed yesterday in The Tribune, is the blackest charge ever placed against an American President and his administration. Once or twice in the history of this Republic charges of graft and peculation have come close to intimates of the White House. Never before in our history did a President maneuver this country into a war for which it was unprepared, and then, thru insouciant stupidity or worse, permit the enemy to execute a surprise attack costing the lives of 3,000 Americans, an attack of which he and his cabinet members had substantial forewarning 24 hours before.

That is the indictment. Let the defendants plead to it. The principal defendant is dead. So are the 3,000 who fell on that Dec. 7. In justice to them, and in justice to all of their quarter of a million fellows in arms who have given their lives since, all of the facts must be placed in the public record.

It is the duty of Congress to get those facts. It is the duty of President Truman to cooperate with Congress. He has by now, we hope, repented his attempt the other day to indict the whole American people for Pearl Harbor, as a means of cloaking the disgrace of the man who deceived him, among others, as to what happened.

One fact must be remembered concerning the reports of the army and navy boards of inquiry which Mr. Truman made public the other day. Those boards were appointed while President Roosevelt was still commander in chief of the army and navy. They did a courageous and conscientious job of investigation which brought out many facts theretofore concealed, but they were not permitted to tell the whole truth. Nowhere in either of their reports was there a single mention of the commander in chief —the commander in chief who delighted not only in ignoring his constitutional civilian advisors, but likewise in overruling his military and naval advisors in military and naval matters of the highest importance.

The fact that the boards of inquiry were directed to suppress the evidence which Mr. Flynn has now disclosed, is clearly stated in their own reports. The navy board said, "The details of this information are not discussed or analyzed in these findings, the court having been informed that their disclosure would militate against the successful prosecution of the war."

Note that the veterans of the court, veteran and capable naval officers of high rank, did not on their own motion say that disclosure of this information would hamper prosecution of the war. They said, "The court having been informed." In other words, higher authority ordered them to lay off.

The senile secretary of war, however, spilled the beans in the self-serving statement by which he attempted to clear himself. Mr. Stimson said:

"Information was received by the war department on December 6, 1941, as to what the Japanese reply to the settlement overtures of the United States would be and that this reply indicated an immediate severance of diplomatic relations."

"Immediate severance of diplomatic relations" is a circumlocution for "war, right now."

That is the evidence that Mr. Flynn developed in his report. Even now a censorship retained for purely political ends forbids disclosure of how the United States obtained this information.

A bill now pending in Congress would inflict 10 years' imprisonment on any one who disclosed such information without the

136

permission of, among others, Mr. Stimson, who is so deeply implicated in the scandal.

Mr. Flynn gave such details as can be told, yesterday. This is the timetable of the final 16 hours in which the last chance to save the lives of the Pearl Harbor victims was fumbled away by the incompetents in Washington. At 10 p.m. on Dec. 6, 1941, the text of the Japanese note severing relations with the United States was placed on the desk of President Franklin D. Roosevelt. The late Secretary Knox read it that night. Secretary Stimson has confessed that the War Department had the information. Knox informed Secretary Hull.

The Japanese note, it must be remembered, was not delivered until the following afternoon when Jap planes were already blasting Pearl Harbor. Mr. Roosevelt and his advisors had it the night before. Its language was unmistakable. It was a declaration of war. What did they do?

They all went to bed.

Secretary Hull called a conference for 10 a.m. the next day, Dec. 7. Furthermore, Lt. Comdr. Kramer of the navy, who was to attend that conference, was instructed not to give his copy of the ultimatum to Adm. Stark until the next morning. Adm. Stark was chief of naval operations. He was censured by the navy board for not warning Adm. Kimmel at Pearl Harbor. His superiors didn't tell him what was going on. The record is confused as to whether Gen. Marshall, chief of staff, had the information that evening. A subordinate officer first testified that he delivered the message to the secretary of the general staff for transmission to Gen. Marshall on Dec. 6, but later changed his testimony and said that the only person to whom he gave this information was the duty officer at the state department.

One thing was missing from the information available to the President and his secretaries of the day before Pearl Harbor. That was the hour at which the Japs' declaration of war was to be delivered. That information became available at 10:20 a.m. on Sunday, two and three-quarters hours before the first bomb fell on Pearl Harbor. Lt. Comdr. Kramer made a brilliant surmise upon the basis of this final information. He gave Secretary Knox a memorandum pointing out that 1 p.m. Washington time was the hour of sunrise over Honolulu, the ideal hour for a surprise bombing attack.

Adm. Stark recognized that the Japanese note meant war. He

cried, "I must get word to Kimmel at once." The word never went thru. Gen. Marshall's warning to Gen. Short in Hawaii, for unexplained reasons, went by slow commercial communications channels. It was delivered after the attack.

In one of the most crucial hours of our history our leaders, military and civilian, were found to be fumbling and incompetent.

And where was Mr. Roosevelt? He apparently did not even consider it necessary to attend the conference of cabinet members called by Mr. Hull.

That afternoon he was playing with his stamp collection, secluded in his study, with the telephone shut off.

Waiting to be surprised.

The

FINAL SECRET

of

PEARL HARBOR

by

John T. Flynn

THIS DOCUMENT reveals, for the first time, the hitherto carefully guarded secret of Pearl Harbor. In the TRUTH ABOUT PEARL HARBOR—a pamphlet—published last October, the Author told what could be told then. Now that the war is over the whole amazing story can be given to the world. Now the reader can learn why Kimmel and Short were never tried; who ordered the suppression of the evidence and who was the guilty author of the great disaster.

Published by
JOHN T. FLYNN
15 E. 40th Street, New York City

Foreword

In October, 1944, I published an account of the Pearl Harbor episode under the title of THE TRUTH ABOUT PEARL HARBOR. There I brought together such material as could be proved at that time. Now that the war is over it is possible to add many darkly hidden facts which can be fully substantiated. The record of this episode was suppressed by President Roosevelt. Many men, however, were witnesses to these events. They have written books, magazine and newspaper articles and letters. Official reports now published contain other segments of the story. A fraction found here, another there, patiently put together, create for us a mosaic which affords us now a complete picture of the scene.

I know, of course, there are those who defend the present order in this country who will object that it is wrong to rake up these old embers now that two of the chief actors—Roosevelt and Knox—are dead. My reply is that they prevented the discussion of them while they lived. I must add also that if they are dead, so are the more than 3000 men who perished in Pearl Harbor on that tragic day. And, if Roosevelt and Knox are dead, Kimmel and Short still live and still suffer under the weight of odium loaded on them by the late President; are still silenced by his orders which deprive them of the right to speak up in their own defense; and are still entitled in a country which loves justice to their day in court. The publication of the watered reports of the Army and Navy Boards render this revised pamphlet necessary.

I must repeat here what I said as preface to the former account which I offered of this case, namely that I did not get or seek information from Admiral Kimmel or General Short or their counsel. I meticulously avoided them in order not to add this embarrassment to the injustices which they have already endured. The facts reported here, however, are beyond dispute. If Congress desires the proofs it can obtain them without any difficulty whatever. The American people are entitled to those proofs.

JOHN T. FLYNN.

New York City, September, 1945.

Second Edition: Revised

The Final Secret of Pearl Harbor

By John T. Flynn

On Wednesday, August 29, 1945, President Truman gave out the reports of the Army and Navy Boards directed by Congress to investigate the responsibility for the great disaster of December 7, 1941, at Pearl Harbor. These Boards had filed their reports nine months ago. Under the pretext that issuance of them would disclose important military secrets President Roosevelt suppressed them. But President Truman has not by any means given out the whole story. Portions of it are still suppressed. He says they will never be given out. And that is the simple truth. They will never be given out by this government until Congress compels the government to release all the information which it is hiding from the people and which it hopes to hide from history.

The Roberts Report—which was also doctored before being released—blamed Admiral Kimmel and General Short for the defeat. Now the two Army and Navy reports expand the guilt to cover General Marshall, Admiral Stark and former Secretary of State Hull. Marshall and Stark were the Army and Navy chiefs in December, 1941. All the top commanders have now been blamed, plus various lesser commanders. But the greatest commander of all is left out—the COM-MANDER-IN-CHIEF. In the 130,000 words of these findings and comments the name of Franklin D. Roosevelt stands out in almost monumental conspicuousness by its absence. The Army and Navy chiefs, the former Secretary of State and Congress have been blamed and the President of the United States has added to the culprits the 130,000,000 people of the United States. The only person not blamed is Franklin D. Roosevelt, who was running the whole show.

However, in spite of all the suppressions, the story of Pearl Harbor is known. And here I propose to tell it. Put in plain terms the tragedy of Pearl Harbor was the dark fruit of three incredible blunders. First in importance was the manner in which the crisis was managed. The second blunder was the bottling of the fleet in Pearl Harbor. The third was the stripping of the defenses of Pearl Harbor. It was Roosevelt who personally managed the whole crisis. It was Roosevelt who bottled the fleet in Pearl Harbor. It was Roosevelt who stripped the base of its defenses. First then, let us look at the crisis as it developed in Washington. Let us see it now in the light of the facts which this government has hidden and which I will now reveal publicly for the first time.

We shall have to look at two battlefields. One was the Pacific, where Kimmel and Short brooded week after week over their deplorable condition, begging for more weapons, fighting against the inroads made on what they had and living almost completely in the dark as to what was happening in that vast, mysterious Pacific world in which they found themselves. We shall look upon that battle-field later.

THE JAPANESE MILITARISTS
DECIDE ON WAR WITH THE UNITED STATES

There was another battlefield. It was mostly in the private apartment of Secretary of State Hull to which the Japanese Ambassador Nomura paid many calls between April and December of 1941. Japan's ruthless policy of conquest had brought her into deep water. The United States, Britain and the Dutch East Indies had cut off all trade with her. Without the iron, oil,

Roosevelt Maneuvers for a Crisis

cotton, rubber and other critical materials from these sources she could not continue the war in China. The situation became desperate. One party—the militarists—was for seizing the Dutch East Indies which would solve the supply problem. But that would mean war with England and—almost certainly —with the United States. The Counsellor of the American Embassy in Tokio

3

had so informed the Japanese Foreign Office. Nevertheless the extremists were for the desperate try. The other party—the moderates, led by the Japanese Premier Konoye—was for making the best terms possible with the United States and getting out of the China affair as best they could. Admiral Nomura was sent to the United States as Ambassador to see what could be done. From April to the end he sat with Cordell Hull, a few times with the President. They argued endlessly. Then on November 16 he was joined by Ambassador Kurusu to assist in the delicate crisis.

There is no space here to follow these conferences. If you will read the official reports of them you will see that as the situation in Japan became more and more desperate, the existing government was willing to make more and more concessions. But the War Party became more and more pressing at home for war. It was a race between the Moderates to get an agreement in Washington and the Warrior Agitators to produce a crisis in Japan. You will see also that President Roosevelt was not going to make any agreement that the Japanese could accept. The talks got nowhere.

Then on October 14 the Moderates lost in Japan. The War-mongers won. The Konoye ministry fell and General Tojo became premier. The President knew that would happen and he knew there could be only one result—a Japanese attack on the Dutch Indies. But there was also the possibility—even probability—that Japan would attempt to deal with England first—would try to reduce Singapore and perhaps attack us in the Philippines. He knew, as he steadfastly refused to hasten the negotiations, that he was producing a situation that could end only with an attack by Japan. Why did he want Japan to attack?

By skillful maneuvers and impossible promises he had brought the country far toward war. From benevolent neutrality, selling to the Allies for cash, he had moved to "Aid-short-of-war"; then to the "Aid-at-the-risk-of-war" frame of mind. By October the once "Aid-short-of-war" group was publishing full-page ads demanding an immediate declaration of war. Senator Pepper, a White House spokesman, said the President had drawn a line and that when Japan moved over it he would start shooting. The President was ready for the final act—the act of open war. Two influences restrained him. His generals and admirals told him we were not ready. Most important was the promise he had made to the American people—solemnly given and repeated—not to send their sons into foreign war *unless attacked.* He did not mind violating that pledge. He merely feared the political effect of the violation. Alsop and Kintner, White House columnist pets, had written a short time before that *"He* (Roosevelt) *does not feel he can openly violate them* (his pledges). *But he can get around them the smart way."* They explained this meant getting the Germans to shoot first. Then he could shoot back. But it was now clear to him that the Germans were not going to shoot first. But now the Japanese were about to do so. If they could be provoked to attack, his problem would be solved. He would then be in the war safely—not only against Japan but "all the way," as he triumphantly announced in his speech to Congress after the attack.

In Japan the war makers were in a desperate hurry. In the United States, Roosevelt, for some reason, became impatient of delay. So much so that *he actually considered sometime before November 14 an invasion of China which would have put us at war with Japan.* He proposed it to the Army and Navy staffs. They dissuaded him because we were not ready. So he waited a little longer —babying the Japanese along, but making it plain that they would get no agreement save by an abject surrender—terms which he knew no Japanese government would dare accept. He did not have long to wait. By November 14 the sands were running fast, as Grew had warned. Something had happened which put the play irrevocably in Roosevelt's hands. This is the event or series of events which have remained locked up in the keeping of the very Inner Circle of the White House. When you read of these you will know why the White House has concealed the truth from the world.

4

THE BREAKING OF THE JAPANESE
CODE SEALS THEIR DOOM

The hour of Fate had arrived in Tokio. But the bedevilled ministers seemed terrified at the appalling folly they were being driven to commit by the violent opinion-makers of Japan. The Japanese High Command began to move their war machine into position. Their plans were made. They had to have the great Dutch islands. That-meant they had to paralyze Britain. But that in turn meant they must, if possible, strike a crushing blow at the United States before she could throw her weight into the struggle. The blow was obvious. This country's naval strength—all the battleships which were the core of her Pacific sea power—were tied up at Pearl Harbor. Some madman had done that surely, they must have thought. But there were the great ships like ducks on a pond waiting for the hunter. Everything depended on the United States leaving the rich target there for the Jap hunters. It was a giant gamble. But a safe one, as we will see, because in the White House sat a President who was satisfied that he knew it all. He had a plan too. And he had made sure, as we shall see, that those battleships and their auxiliary ships would remain quite still and immobilized in the great shooting gallery. But while the Japanese prepared for this gamble, frightened at the peril of waking the still awkward and stupidly led giant America into action they sent the astute Kurusu to Washington to join Nomura in a last effort to get a settlement. Kurusu arrived in Washington on November 16. But by that time the die was cast.

A Gift from the Gods

But now a gift from the gods had been put into Roosevelt's hands. The British government had broken one Japanese code. It proceeded to hand over to the State Department the messages between Tokio and various foreign representatives which it intercepted. Roosevelt now could know what the Japs were saying among themselves. November 4, Roosevelt knew the Japs would yield no more as he had an intercepted dispatch from Tokio saying: "International situation makes any further compromise in this matter impossible." On November 5 an intercepted Tokio dispatch to Washington said: "Signing of any U. S.-Japanese agreement must be completed by November 25." And the Ambassadors were urged by the government to "save Japanese-U. S. relations from chaos." November 6 another intercepted dispatch notified Nomura that Kurusu was coming and that this was the "Last hope of the negotiations." Therefore on November 6, Roosevelt knew that the Japanese were playing their last card; that they would make no further concession and he knew also the very date they had set for action—November 25.

Kurusu seemed to realize quickly enough that he was bucking his head against a stone wall. Troubled by the onrushing deadline he must have appealed to Tokio for more time. Nomura also appealed to the Japanese government. He said in an intercepted dispatch that he *"doubted the wisdom of aggressive action."* Then on November 22 came a dispatch intercepted by the British saying the deadline had been changed to November 29. But it added: *"This time we mean business. Deadline absolutely cannot be changed. After that things will automatically begin to happen."*

What was going to happen? All this information was in the hands of Hull and Roosevelt. Nothing that could happen could surprise them—save undoubtedly the point of the first assault.

Roosevelt Turns the Screw

After being dissuaded from the Chinese invasion project, and seeing the posture of affairs in Japan, the President decided to bring matters to a head. He did not know where the Japanese would launch their attack. It might be on Singapore or some Dutch or British island. In that case he had committed himself—though no one knew it—to join the British in the war on Japan. But that was not an ideal arrangement. His opponents could still insist the United States was not attacked. He was apprehensive about the political implications. He had just won a battle to junk the Neutrality Act. But it was a tremendous battle and he won by a very narrow majority. The enemies of a war declaration were powerful. What was needed was an outright attack on an American possession. Roosevelt decided, therefore, to issue an ultimatum to the Japanese of such a character that America could not possibly be excluded from the coming assault. He had been discussing it since mid-November.

Then on November 26, Secretary Hull did issue an ultimatum to the Japanese. Now he denies it was an ultimatum. But he cannot escape this charge. Nor can the President escape the fact that when it was proposed, General Marshall and Admiral Stark said: "For God's sake, don't send it. We are not ready." Here is what happened.

November 25, Knox, Stimson, Hull, Marshall and Stark met and went to the President's office. Hull showed a plan for a three-months' truce to be given the Japanese. Stimson said he thought it was so drastic the Japanese would reject it. But apparently the group approved it. Hull said he didn't know whether he would offer it "or kick the whole thing over." The next day Hull handed to the Japanese a very different plan—the ten-point plan. It demanded that the Japanese (1) get out of China, (2) get out of Indo-China and (3) repudiate their treaty with the Axis. The Japanese rightly took this as an ultimatum. And Hull too so regarded it then. On that day—November 26—Stimson telephoned Hull. Stimson wrote in his diary: "He (Hull) told me he had broken the whole thing off. As he put it: 'I have washed my hands of it and it is in the hands of you and Knox, the Army and Navy.' " The next day he told the British Ambassador the same thing. General Marshall and Admiral Stark prepared a joint memorandum to the President urging him not to send an ultimatum because we were not prepared. An attempt is made to get rid of this fact by saying it did not reach the President until the 28th, after he had confirmed the ultimatum to the Japanese Ambassador. The Administration sponsors are asking you to believe that the President, who was supposed to know so much, didn't know this fact—that Marshall and Stark knew it but had never told him before. Of course they had warned him when he talked about an invasion of China around November 14. They met with him constantly. The lack of readiness was widely known. Are we supposed to believe that the irreplaceable Commander-in-Chief alone was ignorant of this fact? When Hull handed that ultimatum to the Japanese he and Roosevelt knew it was all over. They sat down then and waited for "things to happen."

What of our two Commanders at Pearl Harbor, inadequately prepared, and in the dark? It is important to remember that Pearl Harbor was 3,500 miles from the points at which the Japanese were preparing their blow. The reconnaissance of the government on these preparations was not in the hands of Short or Kimmel. Other agencies were responsible for that. These agencies

The Fog at Pearl Harbor

reported to Washington. Kimmel and Short had to depend on Washington entirely for their information about the international negotiations and the physical preparation of the Japanese for an attack.

They were not getting information. Here is an example. As far back as July 26, Kimmel wrote Stark asking to be informed of the plans of the government if the Japanese attack the Maritime Provinces and England declares war on her. July 31, Stark wrote another naval officer making an amazing confession. He—Chief of Naval Operations, charged with the plans for eventual war—wrote that he could not get an answer to Kimmel's question, that when he advances it to Roosevelt all he gets is a "smile or 'Betty, please don't ask me that.' " As late as October, Kimmel has not yet been able to get an answer to his question. There is no answer until November 14, when the fuse is already lighted. Then Admiral Stark wrote him saying: "Just what we will do in the Far East REMAINS TO BE SEEN." He was never informed what the U. S. would do in case of war between Japan and Britain in the Pacific. On November 25, after Stark knew an ultimatum would be sent, that the war was only a few days off, he notified Kimmel that the possibility Kimmel had been worrying about was now about to happen, that the Japanese were about to advance in Indo-China, Thailand and the Burma Road most likely. But as to what we will do, he writes a sentence almost beyond belief, unparalleled in the annals of grand strategy: "I WILL BE DAMNED IF I KNOW WHAT THE UNITED STATES WILL DO—ANYTHING OR NOTHING."

The President knew without delay the Japanese reaction to his ultimatum. On November 28 a coded Japanese message intercepted by the British said that "negotiations are ruptured," that the United States proposals are humiliating but that Nomura and Kurusu are not to give the impression that negotiations are off. On November 30, an intercepted code message from Tokio to the Japanese Ambassador in Berlin directs him to notify the German government that *U. S.-Japanese relations are ruptured and that war may break with a clash. May come quicker than anyone dreams with the* ANGLO-SAXON POWERS. And the following day a British intelligence report came that the Japanese carriers had left the home waters.

What were Kimmel and Short told about all this? Literally nothing. Marshall was not in Washington. He left on the 27th to watch army maneuvers in North Carolina. Stimson, acting as Chief of Staff, sent Short a brief message. He called it a war warning. He said negotiations with Japan had ended—thus adopting the interpretation of Hull's note as an ultimatum which would be rejected. But he did not say we had given Japan an ultimatum. He said an aggressive move was expected in a few days. He warned "the United States desires Japan to commit the first overt act." He said: "Prior to hostile action you are directed to undertake such reconnaisance and other measures as you deem necessary, *but these measures should be carried out so as not to alarm the civil population or disclose intent. Report measures taken.*" The whole message was cryptic and inadequate. But this was the fault of Stimson, not Marshall. Next day, Short, who was told to report what he was doing, sent a long message describing in detail the measures he had taken. The Army-Navy plan for defense of Hawaii called for three different types of action—called Alerts. Alert No. 1 was preparation against internal sabotage. Alert No. 2 was mobilization against external attack. Alert No. 3 was a signal for battle positions, when attack begins. Short put into effect Alert No. 1—against sabotage and internal disorder. He had been warned several times about this. He had been warned that all Japanese movements indicated an attack thousands of miles from Pearl Harbor. During the next ten days, though he reported his course, he received no word from Washington ordering a different one.

Why the alert against sabotage, instead of against external air or submarine attack? The reader must have this very clearly in mind. Hawaii had 160,000 Japanese living there. It swarmed with Japanese spies. While the General Staff felt certain the attack would come at least 3,000 miles from Hawaii, they were profoundly frightened lest an internal movement of suicide Japanese patriots would destroy planes and essential installations, crippling the base. Protection against sabotage called for a very different arrangement than from external attack. Short, and all his officers, were certain that is what the High Command indicated and he felt they knew more of the whole Pacific situation than he did. Kimmel, too, was warned not to do anything that would excite the civil population. Whatever he did must be done secretly. Both were warned not even to let their own officers in on these facts save where essential. And they were told "hostilities would begin soon"—but against the Kra Peninsula, Guam, Singapore, Malay.

What was Kimmel doing? It is forgotten that Kimmel's fleet was not there to protect Pearl Harbor. The Harbor was there merely as a fuel and supply base for it. That fleet had a task assigned to it in case of war. The protection of the base would be the duty of the army and the base naval installations. We do not know what the task assigned to Kimmel was. But it is certain that had the

7

Japanese overlooked Pearl Harbor and struck at the Philippines or Singapore alone, Kimmel and his fleet would have been off to sea instantly. Kimmel was preparing for the war task assigned to him, not merely for the protection of Pearl Harbor. We must also bear in mind that after November 27, General Short never received another message giving him any information about the international situation. That is difficult to believe, but it is true. And, we must ask, why was Short told to alert against sabotage while MacArthur in the Philippines was told to alert all out against instant attack?

Roosevelt, the Commander-in-Chief, who was now assured of the attack which would bring him safely into the war, went off to Warm Springs to enjoy the Thanksgiving holiday.

We now come to the night before Pearl Harbor in Washington. The President had returned from Warm Springs because of the crisis. The Japanese envoys had held during the week several meaningless sessions with the State Department. But the formal answer of the Japanese government to the ultimatum had not come.

The Night before Pearl Harbor

But Roosevelt knew what it would be. The stage is all set for the attack on British or, better still, British and American territory in the Pacific. The scenery is beautifully arranged. The President is widely advertised as seeking peace. That night at nine o'clock he sends a dramatic message to Hirohito appealing for peace. He knows this to be as futile as the breeze around the White House grounds. The Japanese navy is putting to sea; Japanese troops are pouring southward. The intercepted codes, of which the public knows nothing, have told the full story.

Luck now played again into Roosevelt's hands. Our Army Intelligence Service broke the Japanese code and learned what they were saying among themselves. On that fateful battle eve it got possession of a document of extraordinary importance. You will recall that the next day—Sunday—the Japanese asked for an appointment at 1 P.M. with Hull. They arrived a little late—when the bombs were falling on Hawaii—and presented a note breaking off relations with us. The incident has been presented to us in shockingly false colors. We were told how the President was in his study on Sunday for a day of rest, confident nothing would happen after his appeal the night before to Hirohito not to precipitate war. He was chatting with Harry Hopkins and fiddling with his stamp collection, while Mrs. Roosevelt entertained in another quarter one of her innumerable groups of uplifters. Then—all of a sudden—out of a clear sky, came news of the attack on Pearl Harbor. It's a goodly picture, but utterly fraudulent. That is not the way things happened. The preceding night— Saturday—the government had got hold of the text of that very document which the Japanese would present the next day. It went to Mr. Roosevelt at 10 P.M. Hull, Knox and Stimson had it. They knew now what was to happen. Hull telephoned Knox and Stimson to meet him next morning for a conference at 10. Consider the situation that night. The President and his three aged and slow-moving cabinet members knew everything—all save the hour and point of attack. Far out in the Pacific the blow would fall. What, in the name of simple common sense, would men of ordinary intelligence do? They knew at that very moment the Japanese ships and planes and subs and troops, under cover of darkness, were moving to their appointed targets. They knew that out in that vast Pacific were two commanders, wretchedly equipped, depending solely on them for information. Would you not suppose the very first act would be to notify General Marshall and Admiral Stark and then, instantly, Admiral Kimmel and General Short? Would you not think that if Marshall and Stark were not in their offices, they were to be hunted through the town, roused from their slumbers to give them this tremendous news? No. The old gentlemen called a conference among themselves for the next day and went home for the slumbers so essential in their advanced years. The President had the news at 10 P.M. He, too, did nothing. Worse than this, a naval aide was told not to give Admiral Stark his copy of the Japanese note until next morning. Why? I think Congress ought to ask for some explanation of this.

The next morning—Sunday—Admiral Stark, because of the tense situation, went to his office. There he found the now completed copy of the Japanese note. "My God!' he cried, "This means war. I must get word to Kimmel at once." For some reason that word did not go at all. Another Japanese code message arrived and was decoded. By 8:20 A.M. the text was in hand.

December the Seventh, 1941
It gave the hour at which the envoys were to present their note to Secretary Hull. The hour was 1 P.M. Washington time. Just as it was decoded another message was intercepted. It advised the twelve Japanese consuls in the United States that Japan was breaking with this country. All were hurried to Knox, Stimson and the President. They were in the hands of Hull's conference at 11 A.M. The bombs would not fall on Pearl Harbor for another two and three-quarters hours.

Lieut. Com. Kramer gave a memorandum to Secretary Knox of trancendent importance. The memorandum pointed out that 1 P.M. Washington time was sunrise over Honolulu and dark night at Manila. Sunrise would be the moment for air attack. As a surprise attack was indicated, the hour of presenting the dispatch indicated an air attack on Pearl Harbor. In other words, we faced an air attack on Pearl Harbor in a little over two hours.

Can we believe that, thus warned, the High Command in Washington, on the edge of such a precipice, would not with whatever speed science had yet devised get this tremendous news and its implication to the Commanders in Hawaii? Instead the three aging secretaries sat down to a conference. General Marshall did not get the news until 11:25 A.M. He then sent a warning message to General Short. There was yet an hour and three-quarters before the explosion. The most precious hour and three-quarters the War Department had ever lived through. Time to get many of the ships in motion. Time to get every available man mobilized. Time to get every available plane off the ground. General Marshall had a scrambler phone which would reach Short instantly. He had also the Navy's powerful short-wave transmitter. Instead of using these he sent the message to General Short by commercial radio at or near 12:18 P.M. Washington time. That would be 6:48 A.M. Honolulu time. It reached Honolulu at 7:33 A.M. The Japanese planes were at that moment winging to their kill. The message was sent through the streets as the bombs were falling. Thus delayed it reached Army Intelligence office at 11:45 A.M. to be decoded. It was delivered to General Short at 2:58 P.M., hours after the great base had been destroyed. Why did not General Marshall use the government's short-wave apparatus? Why did he not use his scrambler phone which would have put this information in the hands of General Short from two and a half to an hour and a half before the attack? His explanation to the Roberts Commission was that he was afraid it might be intercepted. What difference? If intercepted the Japs would merely know what they knew already. But Short would have known it also,

THE PLOT TO
RUIN THE COMMANDERS

While the American public was still stunned by the news of the Pearl Harbor attack, three ideas were promptly fed to the people by the government. One was that the damage was slight. The second was that Kimmel and Short were responsible. The third was that the President was taken completely by surprise. Naval Secretary Knox, after a quick visit to Hawaii, returned and

The Losses Were Small
told us we had lost one battleship, the *Arizona*, three destroyers, a mine layer and an old target ship. Some others were damaged. But the balance of the fleet, he said, including battleships, carriers, heavy and light cruisers, destroyers and submarines were at sea seeking contact with the enemy. Newspapers praised his

9

frankness and the President for making good on his promise of "full information." But this statement was a carefully phrased falsehood. The Secretary juggled with the word "lost." Few ships, indeed, were permanently lost beyond ultimate salvage. But they were lost utterly so far as having any striking power against the enemy was concerned.

The majestic Pacific Fleet had been put out of action as an effective sea weapon. We had eight battleships in Pearl Harbor. The *Arizona* was blown up. The *Nevada,* with a hole in her side, was settled in the mud. The *California* lay on her side. The *West Virginia,* torpedoed six times, rested on the bottom. The *Pennsylvania* and *Maryland* were badly bombed. The *Oklahoma* sank on her side in the shallow water. Three cruisers were badly bombed. Three destroyers were sunk. A large drydock was destroyed. The *Utah* and the *Ogalala* were sunk. The Army and Navy had had nearly 5000 casualties. They lost 197 planes. In time nearly all of these vessels were reclaimed. A few were out in a month. But generally the damage had not been repaired until the Japanese had completed the conquest of the Philippines, Malay and Singapore and much of the rich Indies of the British and Dutch and stood at the gateway to Australia. Why had Knox lied? To deceive the Japanese? Hide from them the extent of our losses? The Japanese knew them only too well. He lied to deceive the American people who had been led to believe the Japanese would be a pushover and who, had they known the full extent of the losses, would have been more clamorous for the heads of the guilty.

Not only was it necessary to conceal the losses. It was necessary to find a scapegoat. Somebody had committed a blunder of historic dimensions. Was it the commanders? Or was it the High Command in Washington? Or was it an even more eminent personage? Of course there had to be an investigation. It was important, therefore, that the investigation be controlled. Congress was

The Attack on Kimmel and Short

clamoring for a congressional inquiry. The Administration blocked that. The President and Knox, along with the Commanders were, pending inquiry, equally suspect. But the President named Knox to do the investigating. Meantime the mud began to fly at Kimmel and Short. Congressman Dingell, New Deal stalwart, let fly in the House. Knowing nothing of the facts he demanded that Kimmel and Short be court-martialled. New Deal newspapers took up the cry. Stories were told of how most of the sailors and marines were ashore after a Saturday night drunk, how all the officers even, were sleeping off the fatigue of late Saturday night parties, how Short and Kimmel themselves were at late parties and of how the two commanders, divided by professional jealousies, seldom spoke to each other and conferred but little about the defense of the island.

In five days Knox was back with the inevitable "report." Of course Knox pointed no accusing finger either at himself or the President. He said: "The United States services were not on alert against the surprise attack. The fact calls for a full investigation which will be initiated immediately by the President."

An indignant outcry broke out against the smeared officers in Congress. Then came the "investigation." The President named a five-man commission. Four were officers who could be depended on not to blame the War and Naval Secretaries or the President. But Justice Roberts was a Republican. This was a master stroke. What the public overlooked was that Roberts had been one of the most clamorous among those screaming for an open declaration of war. He had doffed his robes, taken to the platform in his frantic apprehensions and demanded that we immediately unite with Great Britain in a single nation. The Pearl Harbor incident had given him what he had been yelling for—America's entrance into the war. On the war issue he was one of the President's most impressive allies. Now he had his wish. He could be depended on not to cast any stain upon it in its infancy.

His commission went to Pearl Harbor and investigated. But it was specifically enjoined from investigating the other segments of the story in Washington. Certain essential documents were deliberately concealed from it. It came up with the expected indictment—putting the blame on Kimmel and Short and calling for their court-martial. That fixed the black spot on the Commanders. They were relieved of their posts. They were forbidden to make any statement or enter into any discussion of their innocence. And it was then announced there would be no court-martial. The black spot was fastened on the two helpless victims to stay. The White House took over the management of the whole affair. Army and Naval officials, when asked for statements, said: "The White House is doing the talking." And it did none. It wanted to forget the case. It said: "Let's get on with the war."

From time to time voices rose in Congress to ask some degree of justice for the accused men. Finally Congress, by resolution, ordered the Army and Navy to make formal inquiry of the indicted officers. Boards were named in each Service and the inquiries were made. The Boards reported to their Army and Navy Secretaries in November, 1944. The reports were suppressed by the President on the pretense that military safety required it. Now nine months later President Truman, without knowing enough of the whole intrigue, has given out the reports when it is realized that an angry Congress is about to demand them. The reports have been subjected to alterations and deletions. Kimmel and Short are again smeared and with them Hull, Marshall and Stark. The reports still withhold the gravest facts—those revealed here. And Kimmel and Short, thus dishonored, are still denied a court martial and even a chance to speak up in their defense.

The next bead in the bracelet of defense of the Administration has been that the Army and Navy and the President himself were taken completely by surprise. While they look upon this as a defense for themselves, they apparently do not think it a defense for Kimmel and Short. The theory, endlessly repeated by radio and press, is that we were at peace, that we were actually negotiating for a peaceful settlement and that the President was waiting in complete security for the Japanese answer to his last proposal for peace when, out of a clear sky, the bombs began to fall on Pearl Harbor.

The Surprise Attack

Here is the government's whole case. Our government, while trying to induce Japan to enter upon a peaceful settlement, was taken by carefully studied surprise. But, notwithstanding the surprise, that Government had adequately warned Kimmel and Short of the attack which it did not expect; the Admiral and General did not put their commands on the alert required, and as a consequence the great naval base was exposed to the full fury of the Japanese treachery.

THE FICTION OF
PEACE BEFORE PEARL HARBOR

There is a story of profound importance yet to be told about the state of peace so far as America was concerned before Pearl Harbor. Certainly we had not declared war. But we had sent an army across the sea to Iceland to join the British army there; we had been sending arms, ammunition and destroyers and planes as a gift to Britain and France and China. We had been with our warships hunting down German submarines for British planes and even bombing them. On November 23, W. Averill Harriman, the President's agent in London, said: "The United States Navy is shooting the Germans—German submarines and aircraft at sea." And on September 20, 1941, a dispatch from Hyde Park reported that "More than half of the United States Navy is forced to remain in the Pacific at a time *when the United States is operating against German and Italian submarines and air raiders in the Atlantic.*" In the Pacific we had cut off all shipments and trade of essential materials with Japan and frozen and seized here $130,000,000 of her funds, which Walter Lippmann called "a declaration of economic warfare." We had sent an American military mission to China and an American economic adviser to Chiang Kai-shek. We had sent General Chennault with a large number of American army fliers to China to fight with Chiang's army. At the Atlantic Charter meeting Churchill had urged Roosevelt to send an ultimatum to Japan at once. He had replied saying: "Let me baby her along for another three months."

Mr. Grew, our Ambassador to Tokio, had advised Roosevelt in December, 1940, that the hope of peace had vanished in the East and that it was no longer a question of whether we would have war with Japan but WHEN. The United States must decide whether it should be later or now. And he, Grew, was for NOW. To this on January 21, 1941, Roosevelt replied that he completely agreed with Grew. And a few weeks later Admiral Stark notified Admiral Kimmel that "war with Japan is no longer a question of whether but of when."

There is no room here to discuss these interesting features of what is now a section of history. I do not wish to enter into any consideration here of whether the warlike acts of the President listed above were wise or not. Certainly he was supported in them by large and important groups. I recall them now merely to supply certain features of the international scenery in which the events I am describing took place.

THE BATTLEFIELD AND
WHAT AMERICA HAD ON IT

The Commander of all our military forces was General George C. Marshall, Chief of Staff. The Commander of the Navy was Admiral Harold R. Stark, Chief of Naval Operations. Both, of course, were subject to the President who had by now got into the habit of referring to himself as the Commander-in-Chief. This was not a mere peccadillo. He was already performing directly that function, issuing orders to Stark which the Secretary of the Navy knew nothing of and issuing orders to Marshall without consulting the Secretary of War. His intrusions into the operations of the Navy were more frequent because, while Roosevelt had, under the influence of flatterers who surrounded him, come to think of himself as a master of diplomacy, an expert in political economy, an adept in political manipulation, a wizard in public finance, a profound student of foreign affairs and a military strategist of large dimensions, he regarded himself as little less than a genius in naval organization and direction. This obsession led to the habit of secrecy to avoid the annoyance of hostile advice upon projects he wished to manage.

The Actors in the Drama

Thus in June, when he directed the transfer of naval vessels from the Pacific to the Atlantic, the Secretary of the Navy heard about it first from the Secretary of War. Later, when Hull was asked what had happened to the proposals submitted by the Japanese Premier directly to the President, he said: "I am wondering myself." We have seen that the Chief of Naval Operations could not find out what our plans for the Pacific war were and an American Admiral first learned of certain plans of our government in his theatre from a British admiral. We have seen this headstrong man, surrounded by subservient and obsequious courtiers like Harry Hopkins, Henry Wallace, Sam Rosenman and others, playing secretly the devious game of diplomacy with the Japs and running, often behind the backs of his admirals and generals, segments of a rapidly developing war in two vast oceans.

The point upon which all the forces we have been examining were converging was the small island of Oahu and, in particular, its great naval base near Honolulu—Pearl Harbor. It was supposed to be one of the strongest in the world. The commander of the military establishment in Hawaii was General Walter C. Short. The Pacific Fleet was based at Pearl Harbor and it was under the command of Admiral Husband E. Kimmel. Responsibility for the defense of the island was in the hands of General Short. Admiral Kimmel was expected to give whatever assistance was required from the Navy. But Admiral Kimmel's area of operations

12

extended over the whole Pacific. Further to the West was the Asiatic Fleet based in the Philippines and under the command of Admiral Thomas C. Hart.

Here we must note a fact of great importance. The Pacific Fleet had always been based on our West Coast. Pearl Harbor was a supply and repair base in event of operations in the mid-Pacific. It was Roosevelt who forced the change of bringing the Fleet into Pearl Harbor. In 1940, Admiral Richardson was made Commander-in-Chief of the Pacific Fleet. He was one **Why was the** of the Navy's foremost figures. Since his earliest days, after **Fleet in** leaving Annapolis, he had made the study of Japanese warfare his life work. He was beyond question the Navy's outstanding **Pearl Harbor?** authority upon Pacific naval warfare and Japanese strategy. He was the logical man for the post. As the war clouds darkened over the Pacific he was in the spot for which his whole professional life had been a training. Richardson was ordered to berth the Pacific Fleet in Pearl Harbor. This he refused to do—an act no one but a very distinguished officer could risk. He was ordered a second time and again refused. It was Richardson's belief—and indeed generally supported by the Navy—that the Fleet should never be berthed inside Pearl Harbor where it would be a mark for attack. This was particularly true in such troubled times when the airways of the East were hot with rumors of approaching conflict. What is more Richardson held the belief that Pearl Harbor was the logical first point of attack for the Japanese High Command, wedded as it was to the theory of undeclared and surprise warfare. But Richardson was overruled by Roosevelt, the amateur admiral. Whether Richardson was relieved of his command or resigned in protest I do not know. Certainly he departed from it.

At this point, Admiral Husband E. Kimmel was placed in command. What his views were on the berthing of the Fleet in Pearl Harbor I do not know. But in time he came to look upon the Harbor as extremely vulnerable. He arrived at the conclusion that the Fleet should not be held in Pearl Harbor, that it was a mistake to keep it there for political rather than naval reasons and that the longer it was kept there for political reasons the more difficult it would be to withdraw it without creating further international political repercussions. His advice on this was disregarded, as was Richardson's. He soon learned that neither he nor the Navy Command was running the United States Navy. *This was another terrible blunder responsible for the tragedy at Pearl Harbor.*

In November, 1941, just before the battle, the United States had in its Navy 216 major surface combat ships. The Pacific had always been the home of the greater portion of these vessels. But as the menace grew in Asia where the President looked upon war as certain, he began transferring war vessels to the Atlantic. **Our Battle** By June there were 114 major surface combat vessels in the Atlantic and only 102 in the Pacific. Moreover by this time **Strength in** the President had given away 50 destroyers to the British and these were desperately needed by Kimmel as the crisis neared. **Pearl Harbor** While some of our pulp-paper generals and statesmen were telling the people that Japan was a pushover, the United States, Britain and the Dutch combined had in the Pacific 152 major combat vessels against Japan's 180—perhaps more. The advantage of surprise lay with her and the battlefield was thousands of miles closer to her shores than to ours. I should add that nearly 40 of the vessels we had were laid up for repairs.

Much of the trained personnel had been taken away for service in the Atlantic, leaving the Pacific Fleet manned heavily by raw recruits. These required constant training. Admiral Kimmel wrote to the Navy begging to be kept informed of the international situation so that he could know when to convert from training to service routines.

Despite all this, while the President was ordering Kimmel to "keep ships popping up here and there to worry the Japanese" and Stark was instructing him to make plans for bombing inflammable targets in Japan, the President in May

13

transferred from the Pacific to the Atlantic three battleships, six cruisers, 18 destroyers, six transports with all the trained marines on the West Coast. The Commanders in the Pacific protested without avail. Then in June the President ordered the transfer of three more battleships, four more cruisers, and two squadrons of destroyers to the Atlantic. The naval defenses of the Pacific were being stripped by the President. Stark protested in vain. Then Kimmel went directly to the President and succeeded in dissuading him from this last raid upon his Fleet.

By this time the President's chief adviser on such matters—where he wanted advice—was Harry Hopkins, whose carefully taken policy was always to please the President. On one occasion a distinguished admiral had to go to Mr. Hopkins' bedroom where Hopkins, reclining in his pajamas, gave him a curt "no" to his appeal not to take away any further vessels from his area. Next Admiral King demanded the transfer of more ships from the Pacific to his Atlantic command. Knox was agreeable. It was prevented by Stark's resistance.

The islands' inadequacy in planes was deplorable. The Navy was responsible for long-distance reconnaissance. This meant observations 800 miles all around from Oahu. To do this properly Kimmel would need not less than 180 patrol planes. Kimmel had only 80 or 90 long-distance patrol planes. He had a couple of squadrons of marine planes. He had two carriers—a third was up for repairs.

The Army was much worse off. If the Navy were called away the Army would have to take over long-distance reconnaissance. It should have had 180 B-17's for long-distance patrol. It had six. It had had 12 but was forced to dismantle six to keep the other six supplied with parts for flying. It should have had at least 200 fighter planes. It had a few old P-36's not suitable for combat, ten A-20's good for 600 miles flight (300 miles out and back) and a bunch of old B-18's which could not be used against an enemy without inviting suicide.

Less than ten days before Pearl Harbor, the Army and Navy proposed to ship 50 planes from Hawaii to Wake and Midway and a similar movement of marines and Army personnel. It would have depleted the Army's already pitiful fighter strength by 40 per cent. General Short continually begged for more planes, more men, more detection equipment. Instead of getting reinforcement in the imminent peril of war, the two men had to fight continually to hold what they had. Kimmel too had protested frequently. He advised against "backing into war. If we have decided on war it would be better to take direct defensive action."

The stripping of the naval and airplane and military defenses of Hawaii— particularly of the naval defenses—was another great cause of the disaster at Pearl Harbor. And this was done by the amateur Commander-in-Chief over the advice and protests of his military and naval advisers and of Admiral Kimmel and General Short.

This pathetic tragedy of blunders may be summed up as follows:

1. By January 1, 1941, Roosevelt had decided to go to war with Japan.

2. But he had solemnly pledged the people he would not take their sons to foreign wars *unless attacked.* Hence he dared not attack and so decided to provoke the Japanese to do so.

3. He kept all this a secret from the Army and Navy.

4. He felt the moment to provoke the attack had come by November. He ended negotiations abruptly November 26 by handing the Japanese an ultimatum which he knew they dared not comply with.

5. Immediately he knew his ruse would succeed, that the Japanese looked upon relations as ended and were preparing for the assault. He knew this from the intercepted messages.

6. He was certain the attack would be against British territory, at Singapore

perhaps, and perhaps on the **Philippines** or Guam. If on the Philippines or Guam he would have his desired attack. But if only British territory were attacked could he safely start shooting? He decided he could and committed himself to the British government. But he never revealed this to his naval chief.

7. He did not order Short to change his alert and he did not order Kimmel to take his fleet out of Pearl Harbor, out where it could defend itself, because he wanted to create the appearance of being completely at peace and surprised when the Japs started shooting. Hence he ordered Kimmel and Short not to do anything to cause alarm or suspicion. He was completely sure the Japs would not strike at Pearl Harbor.

8. Thus he completely miscalculated. He disregarded the advice of men who always held that Pearl Harbor would be first attacked. He disregarded the warning implicit in the hour chosen for attack and called to Knox's attention. He disregarded the advice of his chiefs that we were unprepared.

9. When the attack came he was appalled and frightened. He dared not give the facts to the country. To save himself he maneuvered to lay the blame upon Kimmel and Short. To prevent them from proving their innocence he refused them a trial. When the case was investigated by two naval and army boards, he suppressed the reports. He threatened prosecution to any man who would tell the truth.

Now, if there is a shred of decency left in the American people they will demand that Congress open the whole ugly business to the light of day.

History of This Pamphlet

On October 22, 1941, the Chicago TRIBUNE printed an article by John T. Flynn giving the first revealed facts about the mystery that surrounded the persecution of Admiral Kimmel and General Short. It took courage to print that piece. The war was on. Roosevelt was President. His now defunct Gestapo was functioning at top efficiency. Jail was promised to anyone who dared to tell the full story of Pearl Harbor. Few newspapers would dare to defy that threat. Hence after the TRIBUNE published it, the article was reproduced in pamphlet form and soon attained an enormous circulation.

The President and his agents said the story of Pearl Harbor could not be told without revealing critical military information. It was a cunning device. One incident wrapped up in the Pearl Harbor mystery was the breaking of the Japanese diplomatic code by our Army. The whole story, they insisted, could not be made known without giving away that fact. The Japs would then promptly abandon the code through which we were getting important information and we would lose that advantage. Hence they maintained the story of Pearl Harbor must remain buried.

When the war ended that excuse was no longer valid. A wholly new and full account was written in which all the incredible blunders of the President and his Secretaries of War, Navy and State were revealed. Once again the TRIBUNE had the courage to print the story, in spite of the claim in Washington that it could not be done. It appeared Sunday, September 2, 1945. In printing this new story the TRIBUNE said: *"This is the blackest charge ever made against an American President."* This time the Washington *Times-Herald* joined in publishing the story right in Washington. But now once again it is necessary to take to the pamphlet to bring this tale to the eyes of the American people who do not live within the territory served by these newspapers.

The Editor of the TRIBUNE said to his readers when he printed this story:

"Read it. Read it in full. It occupies a good many columns in today's TRIBUNE. That space would not have been made available if the report had not been of such transcendent importance. **WE CALL ON TRUE AMERICANS EVERYWHERE TO JOIN US IN SEEING THAT THE NATION IS TOLD HOW IT WAS CARRIED INTO THE WAR."**

Notes

Chapter 1

1. Lloyd G. Gardner, *Economic Aspects of New Deal Diplomacy* (Boston: Beacon, 1971), p. 328.
2. Edwin Borchard and William Potter Lage, *Neutrality for the United States* (New Haven, Conn.: Yale University Press, 1937), pp. 21–32.
3. George F. Kennan, *American Diplomacy, 1900–1950* (Chicago: University of Chicago Press, 1951), pp. 55–56.
4. Hadley Cantril, *Public Opinion, 1935–1946* (Princeton, N.J.: Princeton University Press, 1951), pp. 966, 971, 973, 975.
5. U.S. Congress, Senate, Nye Committee, *Munitions Industry Supplemental Report on Adequacy of Existing Legislation,* 74th Cong. 2d sess. (Washington, D.C.: U.S. Government Printing Office, 1936), pt. 6, p. 2.
6. U.S. Department of State, *Peace and War: United States Foreign Policy, 1931–1941* (Washington, D.C.: U.S. Government Printing Office, 1943), pp. 266–71.
7. Ibid., pp. 313–14, 355–65; Richard Leopold, *The Growth of American Foreign Policy* (New York: Knopf, 1962), pp. 504–9; Robert A. Divine, *The Illusion of Neutrality* (Chicago: University of Chicago Press, 1962).
8. William L. Langer and S. Everett Gleason, *The Challenge to Isolation, 1937–1940* (New York: Harper and Brothers, 1952), p. 16.
9. *Peace and War,* pp. 383–87.
10. Langer and Gleason, *Challenge to Isolation,* p. 11; James F. Byrnes, *Speaking Frankly* (New York: Harper and Brothers, 1952), p. 6.

11. Robert A. Divine, *Roosevelt and World War II* (Baltimore: Johns Hopkins Press, 1969), pp. 5–6.
12. Divine, *Illusion of Neutrality,* pp. 286–335.
13. Quoted in Charles A. Beard, *American Foreign Policy in the Making, 1932–1940* (New Haven, Conn.: Yale University Press, 1946), p. 316.
14. Robert Sherwood, *Roosevelt and Hopkins* (New York: Harper and Brothers, 1948), p. 201.
15. Wayne S. Cole, *America First* (Madison, Wis.: University of Wisconsin Press, 1953); Michele Stenehjem, *An American First* (New Rochelle, N.Y.: Arlington House, 1976).
16. Walter Johnson, *The Battle Against Isolation* (Chicago: University of Chicago Press, 1944); Mark Chadwin, *The Hawks of World War II* (Chapel Hill, N.C.: University of North Carolina Press, 1968).
17. Cole, *America First,* p. 71; Lawrence Wittner, *Rebels Against War: The American Peace Movement, 1941–1960* (New York: Columbia University Press, 1969), pp. 1–33.
18. "It All Began With FDR," *Newsweek,* December 15, 1975.
19. Maximilian St. George and Lawrence Dennis, *A Trial on a Trial: The Great Sedition Trial of 1944* (New York: National Civil Rights Committee, 1946).
20. Wayne S. Cole, *Charles A. Lindbergh and the Battle Against American Intervention in World War II* (New York: Harcourt Brace Jovanovich, 1974), pp. 125–35.
21. Sherwood, *Roosevelt and Hopkins,* p. 382.
22. Roger Parkinson, *Blood, Toil, Tears and Sweat* (New York: David McKay, 1973), pp. 282–83; Hugh Gibson, ed., *The Ciano Diaries* (Garden City, N.Y.: Doubleday, 1946), p. 398.
23. Winston S. Churchill, *The Grand Alliance* (Boston: Houghton Mifflin, 1951), p. 593.
24. Harold L. Ickes, *The Secret Diary of Harold L. Ickes: The Lowering Clouds, 1939–1941* (New York: Simon and Schuster, 1954), p. 630.
25. William L. Langer and S. Everett Gleason, *The Undeclared War, 1940–1941* (New York: Harper and Brothers, 1953), p. 708; Togo Shigenori, *The Cause of Japan* (New York: Simon and Schuster, 1956), p. 51.
26. Charles A. Lindbergh, *The Wartime Journals of Charles A. Lindbergh* (New York: Harcourt Brace Jovanovich, 1970), p. 561.

27. Cole, *America First,* p. 195.
28. Lindbergh, *Journals,* pp. xii–xiii.

Chapter 2

1. Memoirs of Adm. Royal E. Ingersoll, Columbia University Oral History Project.
2. Testimony of Adm. Royal E. Ingersoll before the Joint Committee on the Investigation of the Pearl Harbor Attack, February 12, 1946, *Hearings Before the Joint Committee on the Investigation of the Pearl Harbor Attack* (hereinafter, *Hearings*), 79th Cong., 1st sess., 39 pts. (Washington, D.C.: U.S. Government Printing Office, 1946), 9:4272–77.
3. Quoted in Antony C. Sutton, *National Suicide: Military Aid to the Soviet Union* (New Rochelle, N.Y.: Arlington House, 1973), p. 81.
4. Winston S. Churchill, *Their Finest Hour* (Boston: Houghton Mifflin, 1949), p. 23.
5. Richard J. Whalen, *The Founding Father* (New York: New American Library, 1964), pp. 309–20; The Earl Jowitt, *Some Were Spies* (London: Hodder and Stoughton, 1954), pp. 40–76.
6. Francis Loewenheim, Harold Langley, and Manfred Jonas, eds., *Roosevelt and Churchill: Their Secret Wartime Correspondence* (New York: Saturday Review Press / E. P. Dutton, 1975), pp. 49–50, 89–96.
7. Sir Llewellyn Woodward, *British Foreign Policy in the Second World War,* 5 vols. (London: Her Majesty's Stationery Office, 1970), 1:261.
8. Ibid., p. 343.
9. Ibid., p. 347.
10. Ibid., p. 351–52.
11. Ibid., pp. 385–6; 2:109.
12. Ibid., 1:394–5.
13. Bruce Bartlett, "Why We Still Have a War Economy," *Reason,* April 1977, pp. 24–28.
14. Warren F. Kimball, *The Most Unsordid Act: Lend-Lease, 1939–1941* (Baltimore: John Hopkins Press, 1969).
15. Leopold, *Growth of American Foreign Policy,* p. 570.
16. Charles A. Beard, *President Roosevelt and the Coming of the War, 1941* (New Haven, Conn.: Yale University Press, 1948), pp. 69–117.
17. *Peace and War,* pp. 737–43.

18. Beard, *President Roosevelt,* pp. 138–42.
19. *Peace and War,* p. 768.
20. Beard, *President Roosevelt,* pp. 142–55.
21. Quoted in Ambassador Joseph C. Grew to Secretary of State, May 18, 1939, *Hearings,* 20:4135–36.
22. Eugene Dooman to Secretary of State, May 23, 1939, ibid., p. 4139.
23. Cordell Hull to the President, July 1, 1939, ibid., p. 4168.
24. Quoted in Herbert Feis, *The Road to Pearl Harbor* (Princeton, N.J.: Princeton University Press, 1950), p. 298; see also Joseph C. Grew, *Turbulent Era: A Diplomatic Record of Forty Years, 1904–1945,* 2 vols. (Boston: Houghton Mifflin, 1952), 2:1272–73.
25. Walter Millis, ed., *The Forrestal Diaries* (New York: Viking, 1951), pp. 90–91.
26. William L. Neumann, "Franklin D. Roosevelt and Japan, 1913–1933," *Pacific Historical Review,* May 1953, pp. 143–53; Paul Schroeder, *The Axis Alliance and Japanese-American Relations, 1941* (Ithaca, N.Y.: Cornell University Press, 1958), pp. 1–28.
27. Sumner Welles, *Seven Decisions That Shaped History* (New York: Harper and Brothers, 1951), p. 80.
28. *Peace and War,* p. 475; Grew, *Turbulent Era,* 2:1212.
29. Grew, *Turbulent Era,* 2:1211–12.
30. U.S. Department of State, *Papers Relating to the Foreign Relations of the United States: Japan, 1931–1941,* 2 vols. (Washington, D.C.: U.S. Government Printing Office, 1943), 2:211–18.
31. Ibid., pp. 218–19.
32. Ibid., pp. 224–25.
33. Testimony of Adm. James O. Richardson before the joint committee, November 20, 1945, *Hearings,* 1:305.
34. George C. Dyer, *On the Treadmill to Pearl Harbor: The Memoirs of Admiral James O. Richardson* (Washington, D.C.: U.S. Government Printing Office, 1973), p. 435.
35. Richardson to Stark, May 22, 1940, *Hearings,* 14:940.
36. Stark to Richardson, May 27, 1940, ibid., p. 943.
37. Richardson to Stark, September 12, 1940, ibid., p. 956.
38. Dyer, *Treadmill,* p. 424.
39. United States–British Staff Conversations Report, March 27, 1941, *Hearings,* 15:1489.
40. Sherwood, *Roosevelt and Hopkins,* p. 273.
41. Ibid., p. 274.
42. Exhibit 114, *Hearings,* 17:2568–600.

43. Chief of Naval Operations to Commander-in-Chief, U. S. Pacific Fleet et al., April 3, 1941, Exhibit 112, ibid., p. 2463.
44. American-Dutch-British Conversations Report, Singapore, April, 1941, Exhibit 50, ibid., 15:1564.
45. Feis, *Road to Pearl Harbor*, p. 170.
46. Parkinson, *Blood, Toil, Tears and Sweat,* p. 282.
47. Ibid., p. 283.
48. Gibson, *Ciano Diaries*, p. 398.
49. Churchill, *Grand Alliance* p. 593.
50. Parkinson, *Blood, Toil, Tears and Sweat,* p. 282.
51. Churchill, *Grand Alliance,* p. 440.
52. Ibid.
53. Winston S. Churchill, *The End of the Beginning* (Boston: Little, Brown, 1943), p. 33.
54. *Peace and War,* pp. 704–5.
55. Robert J. C. Butow, *Tojo and the Coming of the War* (Princeton, N.J.: Princeton University Press, 1961), p. 242.
56. Langer and Gleason, *The Undeclared War,* p. 708.
57. Director, War Plans Division to Chief of Naval Operations, July 19, 1941, *Hearings,* 5:2383.
58. Ibid., p. 2384.
59. Admiral Harold Stark to Sumner Welles, July 22, 1941, ibid., p. 2382.
60. *Foreign Relations,* 2:527.
61. Tokyo to Washington #433, July 31, 1941, Exhibit 1, *Hearings,* 12:9.
62. Quoted in Feis, *Road to Pearl Harbor,* p. 248.
63. *Foreign Relations,* 2:563–65.
64. Feis, *Road to Pearl Harbor,* pp. 271–81.
65. Ibid., p. 298.
66. Joseph C. Grew, *Ten Years in Japan* (New York: Simon and Schuster, 1944), p. 470.
67. *Foreign Relations,* 2:650.

Chapter 3

1. Herbert O. Yardley, *The American Black Chamber* (London: Faber and Faber, 1931), pp. 174–224.
2. Henry L. Stimson and McGeorge Bundy, *On Active Service in Peace and War* (New York: Harper and Brothers, 1948), p. 188.

3. Ronald Clark, *The Man Who Broke Purple* (Boston: Little, Brown, 1977), pp. 138–46; David Kahn, *The Codebreakers* (New York: Macmillan, 1967), pp. 18–26.
4. Clark, *Man Who Broke Purple*, pp. 149–59.
5. Tokyo to Washington #725, November 4, 1941, *Hearings*, 12: 92–93.
6. *Peace and War*, p. 776.
7. Cordell Hull, *The Memoirs of Cordell Hull*, 2 vols. (New York: Macmillan, 1948), p. 1058.
8. Ibid.
9. Tokyo to Washington #727, November 4, 1941, *Hearings*, 12: 96–97.
10. Tokyo to Washington #736, November 5, 1941, ibid., p. 100.
11. Hull, *Memoirs*, p. 1057.
12. Memorandum to the President, November 5, 1941, *Hearings*, 14:1061–62.
13. Diary of Henry L. Stimson, November 6, 1941, ibid., 11:5431.
14. *Peace and War*, pp. 801–2.
15. Hull, *Memoirs*, p. 1069.
16. Exhibit 18, *Hearings*, 14:1109.
17. Tokyo to Washington #812, November 22, 1941, ibid., 12: 165.
18. Hull, *Memoirs*, p. 1074.
19. Diary of Henry L. Stimson, November 25, 1941, *Hearings*, 11: 5433.
20. Statement of Henry L. Stimson before the joint committee, March 1946, ibid., pp. 5421–22.
21. Diary of Henry L. Stimson, November 25, 1941, ibid., p. 5433.
22. Idem, November 26, 1941, ibid., p. 5434.
23. *Peace and War*, pp. 810–11.
24. John Toland, *The Rising Sun* (New York: Random House, 1970), p. 141.
25. Diary of Henry L. Stimson, November 25, 1941, *Hearings*, 11: 5433.
26. Idem, November 27, 1941, ibid., pp. 5434–35.
27. Exhibit 32, ibid., 14:1328.
28. H. Montgomery Hyde, *Room 3603* (New York: Farrar, Straus, 1962), p. 213; William Stevenson, *A Man Called Intrepid* (New York: Harcourt Brace Jovanovich, 1976), p. 299.
29. Diary of Henry L. Stimson, November 27, 1941, *Hearings*, 11: 5434.

30. Memorandum for the President, November 27, 1941, ibid., 14:1083.
31. Exhibit 37, ibid., 14:1329.
32. Testimony of Gen. Walter Short before the joint committee, January 22, 1946, ibid., 7:2935–36.
33. Exhibit 37, ibid., 14:1330.
34. Ibid.; testimony of Gen. Walter Short before the joint committee, January 22, 1946, ibid., 7:2936–37.
35. Top Secret Report of the Army Pearl Harbor Board, ibid., 39:221.
36. Testimony of Capt. Arthur H. McCollum before the joint committee, January 30, 1946, ibid., 8:3396.
37. George Morgenstern, *Pearl Harbor* (New York: Devin-Adair, 1947), pp. 17–18.
38. Toland, *Rising Sun,* pp. 150–54.
39. Grew to Secretary of State, January 27, 1941, *Hearings,* 14:1042.
40. Kimmel to Stark, February 18, 1941, ibid., 16:2229.
41. A. A. Hoehling, *The Week Before Pearl Harbor* (New York: Norton, 1963), pp. 52–70.
42. Stark to Kimmel, March 22, 1941, *Hearings,* 16:2160.
43. Tokyo to Honolulu #83, September 24, 1941, ibid., 12:261; Tokyo to Honolulu #11, November 15, 1941, ibid., p. 262; Tokyo to Honolulu #122, November 29, 1941, ibid., p. 263.
44. Testimony of Capt. Alwin D. Kramer before the joint committee, February 11, 1946, ibid., 9:4196.
45. Testimony of Capt. Arthur H. McCollum before the joint committee, January 30, 1946, ibid., 8:3405.
46. Charles A. Willoughby and John Chamberlain, *MacArthur: 1941–1951* (New York: McGraw-Hill, 1954), pp. 22–23.
47. Tokyo to Honolulu #111, November 15, 1941, *Hearings,* 12: 262.
48. Tokyo to Honolulu #122, November 29, 1941, ibid., p. 263.
49. Testimony of Col. Otis K. Sadtler before the Army Pearl Harbor Board (APHB), October 6, 1944, ibid., 29:2429.
50. Tokyo to Washington #2444, December 1, 1941, ibid., 12: 209; Tokyo to London #2443, December 1, 1941, ibid.; Tokyo to Washington #867, December 2, 1941, ibid., p. 215; Bern to Ankara #2447, December 2, 1941, ibid., p. 216.
51. Testimony of Adm. John Beardall before the joint committee, April 11, 1946, ibid., 11:5284.

52. Sherman Miles to Military Attache, American Embassy, Tokyo, December 3, 1941, ibid., 14:1409.

53. OPNAV to CINCAF, December 2, 1941, ibid., 14:1407.

54. CINCAF to OPNAV, December 2, 1941, ibid., 6:2670–71.

55. Testimony of Adm. Harold Stark before the joint committee, January 2, 1946, ibid., 6:2190.

56. U.S. Naval Institute *Proceedings,* October 1963, pp. 127–29; Kemp Tolley, "The Strange Assignment of the USS *Lanikai,"* U.S. Naval Institute *Proceedings,* September 1962, pp. 71–83; idem, *Cruise of the Lanikai* (Annapolis, Md.: Naval Institute Press, 1973).

57. Testimony of Adm. Royal E. Ingersoll before the joint committee, February 12, 1946, *Hearings,* 9:4252–54.

58. Testimony of Lt. Robert O'Dell before the Clarke Investigation, October 6, 1944, ibid., 34:60; idem before the APHB, October 6, 1944, ibid., 29:2301–3; Merle-Smith to War Department, December 6, 1941, ibid., 34:172.

59. Woodward, *British Foreign Policy,* 2:170–71.

60. Ibid., p. 171.

61. Ibid., p. 180.

62. Memorandum of Conversation, December 5, 1941, *Hearings,* 11:5472.

63. S. Winburn Kirby, *The War Against Japan: The Loss of Singapore* (London: Her Majesty's Stationery Office, 1957), p. 175; Lionel Wigmore, *The Japanese Thrust* (Canberra, Australia, 1957), p. 109; Raymond A. Esthus, "President Roosevelt's Commitment to Britain to Intervene in a Pacific War," *Mississippi Valley Historical Review,* June 1963, pp. 28–38.

64. CINCAF to OPNAV, December 7, 1941, *Hearings,* 14:1412.

65. Winant to Secretary of State, December 6, 1941, ibid., 14:1247; testimony of Sumner Welles, November 24, 1945, ibid., 2:494.

66. Australian Minister for External Affairs to Secretary of State for Dominion Affairs, United Kingdom, ibid., 11:5166.

67. Memorandum for the President, November 29, 1941, ibid., 14:1202; President Roosevelt to Emperor Hirohito, December 6, 1941, *Peace and War,* pp. 829–31.

68. OPNAV to Commanders of all Naval Districts, April 1, 1941, *Hearings,* 14:1395–96.

69. Tokyo to Washington #901, December 6, 1941, ibid., 12:238–39.

70. Testimony of Capt. Arthur H. McCollum before the Hewitt Inquiry, May 14, 1945, ibid., 36:25.
71. Testimony of Comdr. Lester Schulz before the joint committee, February 15, 1946, ibid., 10:4662.
72. Ibid., p. 4663.
73. Testimony of Capt. Arthur H. McCollum before the Hewitt Inquiry, May 14, 1945, ibid., 36:25–27.
74. Exhibit 61, ibid., 15:1640.
75. Report of the Army Pearl Harbor Board, ibid., 39:93–96.
76. Robert A. Theobald, *The Final Secret of Pearl Harbor* (New York: Devin-Adair, 1954).
77. Thomas A. Bailey, *The Man in the Street: The Impact of American Public Opinion on Foreign Policy* (New York: Macmillan, 1948), pp. 11–12.
78. Bruce M. Russett, *No Clear and Present Danger: A Skeptical View of the U.S. Entry into World War II* (New York: Harper and Row, 1972).

Chapter 4

1. Testimony of Adm. James O. Richardson before the joint committee, November 20, 1945, *Hearings*, 1:305; Dyer, *On the Treadmill to Pearl Harbor*, pp. 423–36.
2. See Husband E. Kimmel, *Admiral Kimmel's Story* (Chicago: Regnery, 1955), pp. 11–31; see also Kimmel's letters to Stark, *Hearings*, 16:2225–57.
3. Chief of Naval Operations to Adm. Husband E. Kimmel et al., April 3, 1941, ibid., 17:2463.
4. A photographic copy of this headline may be found between pp. 2820 and 2821, ibid., pt. 6.
5. Exhibit 37, #36, ibid., 14:1406. This same warning was sent to Adm. Thomas Hart in the Philippines, who testified concerning it: "The Asiatic Fleet had to await attack. It could not attack. So, manifestly, the measure was to so dispose ourselves that when the attack came it would inflict as little damage as was possible." Testimony of Adm. Thomas Hart before the joint committee, February 18, 1946, ibid., 10:4812.
6. This was the gist of Admiral Kimmel's defense; see statement of Adm. Husband E. Kimmel before the joint committee, Jan-

uary 15, 1946, ibid., 6:2498–554; see also Kimmel, *Kimmel's Story*, pp. 32–77.

7. Kimmel, *Kimmel's Story*, p. 3.
8. Kimmel to Stark, February 18, 1941, *Hearings*, 6:2227–29; Stark to Kimmel, March 22, 1941, ibid., pp. 2157–60; Kimmel to Stark, May 26, 1941, ibid., pp. 2233–38.
9. Report of the Secretary of the Navy to the President, ibid., 5:2338–45.
10. Frank E. Beatty, "Background of the Secret Report," *National Review*, December 13, 1966, pp. 1261–65. Beatty was Knox's aide.
11. Paul S. Burtness and Warren U. Ober, "Secretary Stimson and the First Pearl Harbor Investigation," *Australian Journal of Politics and History* 14 (Spring, 1968): 24–29.
12. Stimson to Roosevelt, December 16, 1941, *Hearings*, 7:3260.
13. William H. Standley and Arthur A. Ageton, *Admiral Ambassador to Russia* (Chicago: Regnery, 1955), p. 80.
14. Henry L. Stimson Diary, Yale University Library, New Haven, Conn., entry for December 17, 1941.
15. Proceedings of the Roberts Commission, *Hearings*, 24:1306.
16. Standley and Ageton, *Admiral Ambassador*, pp. 80–81.
17. Ibid., p. 82.
18. Ibid.; see also Proceedings of the Roberts Commission, *Hearings*, 24:1307–8.
19. Kimmel, *Kimmel's Story*, pp. 147–48.
20. Ibid.; see also Proceedings of the Roberts Commission, *Hearings*, 22:375.
21. Standley and Ageton, *Admiral Ambassador*, pp. 83–84.
22. Report of the Roberts Commission, *Hearings*, 39:20–21.
23. George C. Marshall to Thomas E. Dewey, September 27, 1944, ibid., 3:1133.
24. Standley and Ageton, *Admiral Ambassador*, pp. 87–88.
25. Testimony of Mr. Justice Roberts before the joint committee, January 28, 1946, *Hearings*, 7:3280.
26. Kimmel, *Kimmel's Story*, p. 149.
27. "Resume of Public Opinion About the Commission to Investigate the Attack at Pearl Harbor," Proceedings of the Roberts Commission, *Hearings*, 24:1288.
28. See U.S. Congress, *Congressional Record*, December 11, 1941, pp. 9656–59.
29. Standley and Ageton, *Admiral Ambassador*, p. 82.

30. Henry L. Stimson to Justice Owen Roberts, January 27, 1942, *Hearings,* 7:3261.
31. Stimson Diary, January 26, 1942.
32. Testimony of Gen. Walter Short before the joint committee, January 25, 1946, *Hearings,* 7:3133–34.
33. Stimson Diary, January 26, 1942; Forrest C. Pogue, *George C. Marshall: Ordeal and Hope, 1939–1942* (New York: Viking, 1966), pp. 435–38.
34. Testimony of Gen. Walter Short before the joint committee, January 26, 1946, *Hearings,* 7:3170.
35. Testimony of Adm. Husband Kimmel before the joint committee, January 16, 1946, ibid., 6:2561.
36. Secretary of the Navy to Kimmel, February 16, 1942, ibid., 17:2731; Stark to Kimmel, February 21, 1942, ibid., p. 2730.
37. See Roland Young, *Congressional Politics in the Second World War* (New York: Columbia University Press, 1956), p. 171.
38. See the two memoranda of events leading up to the congressional investigation of Pearl Harbor by Admiral Kimmel dated June 6, 1946, and November 1966, Husband E. Kimmel Papers, University of Wyoming Library, Laramie, Wyoming (hereinafter, "Kimmel memoranda").
39. Ibid.
40. Ibid.
41. Ibid.
42. Ibid.; Kimmel, *Kimmel's Story,* pp. 130–31.
43. Testimony of Capt. Laurence F. Safford before the Hewitt Inquiry, May 21, 1945, *Hearings,* 36:69. Capt. A. H. McCollum was head of the Far East Section, Office of Naval Intelligence.
44. Kimmel, *Kimmel's Story,* pp. 130–31.
45. Testimony of Capt. Laurence Safford before the Hart Inquiry, April 29, 1944, *Hearings,* 26:387–95.
46. U.S. Congress, *Congressional Record,* June 5, 1944, p. 5342; Young, *Congressional Politics,* pp. 171–72.
47. The Naval Court of Inquiry (NCI) convened on July 24 and held hearings until October 19, 1944. It consisted of Admirals Orin G. Murfin, Edward C. Kalbfus, and Adolphus Andrews. The Army Pearl Harbor Board (APHB) convened on July 20 and held hearings until October 20, 1944. It consisted of Generals George Grunert, Henry D. Russell, and Walter Frank.
48. "Kimmel memoranda."

49. Affidavit of Gen. Sherman Miles before the Clausen Investigation, August 16, 1945, *Hearings,* 35:101.
50. Testimony of Adm. Husband Kimmel before the APHB, August 25, 1945, ibid., 28:946–47.
51. Affidavit of Gen. George Marshall before the Clausen Investigation, August 28, 1945, ibid., 35:104.
52. Report of the NCI, ibid., 39:321.
53. Report of the APHB, ibid., p. 145.
54. Memorandum from Judge Advocate General to Secretary of War, re APHB report, November 25, 1944, ibid., p. 264.
55. See Statement by Secretary Stimson, ibid., 21:4654–61; Fourth Endorsement to Record of Proceedings of Pearl Harbor Court of Inquiry by Secretary Forrestal, August 13, 1945, ibid., 39: 383.
56. James Forrestal Diary, Princeton University Library, Princeton, N.J., entry for August 18, 1945; see also entry for November 22, 1945.
57. Kimmel, *Kimmel's Story,* pp. 160–61; see also Lavender to Kimmel, September 7, 1944, and Kimmel to Rugg, October 19, 1944, Kimmel Papers.
58. Memorandum to Major Clausen from General Cramer, *Hearings,* 35:6–7.
59. See Pogue, *General Marshall,* p. 433.
60. Richardson told this to Kimmel on March 13, 1945, Kimmel to Rugg, March 14, 1945, Kimmel Papers.
61. Kimmel to Rugg, February 1, 1945, ibid.; Kimmel to Rugg, February 12, 1945, ibid.
62. Report of the Hewitt Inquiry, Hearings, 39:456–66; Interview with Adm. Kent Hewitt, Columbia Oral History Project, New York, N.Y., p. 24.

Chapter 5

1. *Congressional Record,* December 11, 1941, pp. 9656–59.
2. Standley and Ageton, *Admiral Ambassador,* p. 82.
3. Young, *Congressional Politics,* pp. 171–72.
4. Rosalie M. Gordon (Flynn's secretary) to Westbrook Pegler, January 18, 1947, Pegler Papers, Herbert Hoover Presidential Library, West Branch, Iowa.

5. John T. Flynn, *The Truth About Pearl Harbor* (New York: privately printed, 1944).

6. J. Loy Maloney to John T. Flynn, October 19, 1944, Flynn Papers, University of Oregon Library, Eugene, Oregon.

7. Editorial, "J'Accuse, 1944," *Chicago Tribune,* October 23, 1944.

8. John Chamberlain, "Pearl Harbor," *Life,* September 24, 1945, pp. 110–20.

9. Marshall to Dewey, September 25, 1944, *Hearings,* 3:1130.

10. Marshall to Dewey, September 27, 1944, ibid., pp. 1132–33.

11. Sherwood, *Roosevelt and Hopkins,* p. 827.

12. Forrest Pogue, *George C. Marshall: Organizer of Victory, 1943–1945* (New York: Viking, 1973), p. 473.

13. Robert A. Divine, *Foreign Policy and U.S. Presidential Elections, 1940–1948* (New York: New Viewpoints, 1974), p. 147.

14. *Human Events,* September 26, 1945. Similar views are found in the *New York Times,* December 9, 1945, and Ernest K. Lindley, "Weighing Evidence: Dewey and Pearl Harbor," U.S. Congress, *Congressional Record,* October 10, 1945, p. A4247. For the view of an advisor who thought Dewey should have told the story, see Upton Close, "Reading the Signs," *New York Journal-American,* September 25, 1945.

15. Kimmel, *Kimmel's Story,* p. 127.

16. Rugg to Ferguson, April 5, 1945, Kimmel Papers, University of Wyoming Library, Laramie, Wyoming.

17. Chief of Naval Operations to Secretary of the Navy, November 3, 1944, *Hearings,* 39:333.

18. U.S. Congress, *Congressional Record,* April 9, 1945, p. 3196; John Chamberlain, "The Man Who Pushed Pearl Harbor," *Life,* April 1, 1946, p. 85; Kimmel to Rugg, April 12, 1945, Kimmel Papers; Kimmel to Yarnell, April 11, 1945, ibid.; Taft to Rugg, April 25, 1945, ibid.

19. Editorial, "Wraps on History," *Washington Post,* April 12, 1945; see also Lavender to Kimmel, April 12, 1945, Kimmel Papers; Kimmel, *Kimmel's Story,* p. 127.

20. U.S. Congress, *Congressional Record,* June 21, 1945, p. 6430.

21. Harry S. Truman, "Our Armed Forces Must Be Unified," *Collier's,* August 26, 1944.

22. *Washington Times-Herald,* August 21, 1944.

23. Forrestal Diary, entry for April 18, 1945.

24. Ibid., entries for August 18 and 29, 1945.

25. *Human Events,* August 22, 1945.
26. John T. Flynn, *The Final Secret of Pearl Harbor* (New York: privately printed, 1945); editorial, "The Indictment," *Chicago Tribune,* September 3, 1945. Both are reproduced in this volume, Appendix Three.
27. *Human Events,* September 5, 1945.
28. Exhibit 181, *Hearings,* 21:4701.
29. U.S. Congress, *Congressional Record,* September 5, 1945, pp. 8338–45; Arthur Krock, "Standards for Investigation of Pearl Harbor," *New York Times,* September 6, 1945; Hanson Baldwin, "Pearl Harbor Inquiry: Open, Fearless Investigation Urged to Glean Data of Value for Future," ibid., September 9, 1945.
30. Flynn to DeWitt Wallace, September 17, 1945, Flynn Papers.
31. *Wall Street Journal,* November 8, 1945.
32. *Hearings,* 1:8.
33. Ibid., 11:5510–11.
34. Ibid., 1:9.
35. U.S. Congress, *Congressional Record—Senate,* November 2, 1945, pp. 10341, 10344.
36. Ibid., pp. 10350, 10356.
37. Flynn to Merwin K. Hart, September 27, 1945, Flynn Papers.
38. William H. Regnery to Flynn, October 23, 1945, ibid.; Cole, *America First,* pp. 22, 32, 195.
39. Lammot DuPont to Flynn, October 12, 1945, Flynn Papers; "Report of P. H. Account from October, 1945 to March 15, 1946," by Helen O'Connor, ibid.
40. See Percy L. Greaves, "The Pearl Harbor Investigations," in Harry Elmer Barnes, ed., *Perpetual War For Perpetual Peace* (Caldwell, Ida.: Caxton, 1953), pp. 448–51.
41. *Hearings,* 3:1372–73, 4:1719–20; Alben W. Barkley, *That Reminds Me* (Garden City, N.Y.: Doubleday, 1954), p. 265.
42. *Hearings,* 4:1586.
43. Ibid., p. 1590.
44. See *U.S. News and World Report,* January 11, 1946.
45. Tokyo to Washington #902, December 6, 1941, *Hearings,* 12: 239–45.
46. Chamberlain, "The Man Who Pushed Pearl Harbor," p. 85.
47. Testimony of Lester Schulz before the joint committee, February 15, 1946, *Hearings,* 10:4662–63.
48. Flynn to Gearhart, July 15, 1946, Flynn Papers.
49. Flynn to Keefe, July 16, 1946, ibid.; Keefe to Flynn, July 18,

1946, ibid.; Keefe's "additional views" may be found in *Report of the Joint Committee on the Investigation of the Pearl Harbor Attack,* 79th Cong. 2d sess. (Washington, D.C.: U.S. Government Printing Office, 1946), pp. 266–266-w; see also Beard, *President Roosevelt,* pp. 345–50.

50. Flynn to Keefe, July 19, 1946, Flynn Papers; see also Flynn to Ferguson, July 19, 1946, ibid.

51. John T. Flynn, "Dec. 7 'Whitewash' Is Congress Scandal," *New York Journal-American,* July 21, 1946; Beard, *President Roosevelt,* pp. 345–50. Flynn finally decided that Gearhart caved in because of a stiff primary fight he was waging, but never did figure out why Keefe defected; see Flynn to Harry Elmer Barnes, April 12, 1951, Barnes Papers, University of Wyoming Library, Laramie, Wyoming.

52. "Pearl Harbor Republicans Knock Out Party's Issue," *P.M.,* July 22, 1946; "GOP Still After A Gem in 'Pearl' Report," ibid.; editorial, "The Pearl Harbor Report," *New York Times,* July 21, 1946.

53. William S. White, "Pearl Harbor End Marked by Dispute," *New York Times,* May 24, 1946; "Ferguson to Let Pearl Harbor Inquiry Drop," *New York Herald-Tribune,* July 22, 1946.

54. For Flynn's later years, see Ronald Radosh, *Prophets on the Right* (New York: Simon and Schuster, 1975), pp. 231–73; see also Richard C. Frey, "John T. Flynn and the United States in Crisis, 1928–1950," (Doctoral dissertation: University of Oregon, 1969).

Chapter 6

1. For details on Safford, see Kahn, *Codebreakers,* p. 10; Ladislas Farago, *The Broken Seal* (New York: Random House, 1967), pp. 41–46, 95–96.

2. Tokyo to Washington #2353, November 19, 1941, *Hearings,* 12:154.

3. Tokyo to Washington #2354, November 19, 1941, ibid., p. 155.

4. CINCAF to OPNAV, November 18, 1941, ibid., 18:3303; Foote to Secretary of State, December 4, 1941, ibid., pp. 3303–4; Thorpe to War Department, December 5, 1941, ibid., p. 3304.

5. Testimony of Alwin D. Kramer before the joint committee, February 6, 1946, ibid., 8:3915.
6. Testimony of Rufus Bratton before the joint committee, February 15, 1946, ibid., 10:4624.
7. Testimony of Leigh Noyes before the joint committee, February 16, 1946, ibid., pp. 4725–26.
8. Testimony of Laurence Safford before the Hart Inquiry, April 29, 1944, ibid., 26:393–94.
9. Idem before the NCI, August 29, 1944, ibid., 33:771–72.
10. Idem before the APHB, October 2, 1944, ibid., 29:2371–72.
11. Ibid., pp. 2373, 2378.
12. Idem before the Hewitt Inquiry, May 21, 1945, ibid., 36:71–74.
13. Testimony of F. M. Brotherhood before the NCI, September 11, 1944, ibid., 33:839–45; idem before the Hewitt Inquiry, May 22, 1945, ibid., 36:88–89; testimony of A. A. Murray before the Hewitt Inquiry, June 9, 1945, ibid., pp. 258–59; testimony of G. W. Linn before the Hewitt Inquiry, May 22, 1945, ibid., pp. 86–87; testimony of A. V. Pering before the Hewitt Inquiry, May 22, 1945, ibid., p. 90.
14. Testimony of Alwin D. Kramer before the NCI, September 13, 1944, ibid., 33:853.
15. Idem before the Hewitt Inquiry, May 22, 1945, ibid., 36:80–81; idem, July 6, 1945, ibid., pp. 339–41.
16. Idem before the joint committee, February 6, 1946, ibid., 8:3939.
17. Laurence F. Safford, "Memorandum of Conversations in Connection with Admiral Hewitt's Investigation of the Pearl Harbor Disaster," July 14, 1945, ibid., 18:3345–46.
18. Report of the Hewitt Inquiry, ibid., 39:456–66.
19. See Laurence F. Safford, "Circumstantial Evidence Pertaining to the Winds Execute Message," October 22, 1945, Safford Papers, University of Wyoming Library, Laramie, Wyoming; idem, "Circumstantial Evidence Pertaining to Transmission of the Winds Message," November 1, 1945, ibid.
20. Safford, "Circumstantial Evidence Pertaining to the Winds Execute Message," October 22, 1945, Safford Papers.
21. Ibid.
22. Testimony of William F. Friedman before the Hewitt Inquiry, June 22, 1945, *Hearings,* 36:306; idem before the Clarke Inquiry, July 31, 1945, ibid., 34:80.

23. Testimony of Isaac Spaulding before the Clarke Inquiry, July 17, 1945, ibid., 34:89–92.
24. Testimony of John T. Bissell before the Clarke Inquiry, August 4, 1945, ibid., pp. 99–102.
25. Testimony of Laurence F. Safford before the APHB, October 2, 1944, ibid., 29:2392.
26. Testimony of Thomas Hart before the joint committee, February 18, 1946, ibid., 10:4797.
27. Top Secret Report of the Army Pearl Harbor Board, ibid., 39:226.
28. Drew Pearson, "Washington Merry-Go-Round," *San Francisco Chronicle*, November 5 and 7, 1945.
29. U.S. Congress, *Congressional Record—Senate*, November 6, 1945, pp. 10431–2; U.S. Congress, *Congressional Record—House*, November 6, 1945, pp. 10445–45. For examples of media interest in the Winds execute, see "Pearl Harbor Mystery: Dispute Over 'Wind' Message," *U. S. News and World Report*, February 15, 1946; John T. Flynn, " 'Wind' Code Key to New Deal Guilt," *New York Journal-American*, December 13, 1945.
30. Testimony of Laurence F. Safford before the joint committee February 1, 1946, *Hearings*, 8:3579–91.
31. Tokyo to Washington #2444, December 1, 1941, ibid., 12:209.
32. *Report of the Joint Committee*, pp. 469–86.
33. Ibid., p. 486.
34. Testimony of F. M. Brotherhood before the Hewitt Inquiry, May 22, 1945, Hearings, 36:89; see also testimony of Leigh Noyes before the joint committee, February 16, 1946, ibid., 10:4732. For a copy of the "false" execute, see Exhibit 142, ibid., 18:3306.
35. Testimony of Leigh Noyes before the joint committee, February 16, 1946, ibid., 10:4728–34.
36. Testimony of Laurence Safford before the joint committee, February 1, 1946, ibid., 8:3686.
37. Testimony of Otis K. Sadtler before the APHB, October 6, 1944, ibid., 29:2430; idem before the Clarke Inquiry, September 16, 1944, ibid., 34:67–68; testimony of Richmond K. Turner before the joint committee, December 20, 1945, ibid., 4:1968; idem before the NCI, September 15, 1944, ibid., 33:885.

38. Testimony of Leigh Noyes before the joint committee, February 16, 1946, ibid., 10:4733–34.
39. Roberta Wohlstetter, *Pearl Harbor: Warning and Decision* (Stanford, Calif.: Stanford University Press, 1962), p. 219.
40. Testimony of Richmond K. Turner before the joint committee, December 20, 1945, *Hearings,* 4:1968; idem before the NCI, September 15, 1944, ibid., 33:885–86.
41. Testimony of Royal E. Ingersoll before the joint committee, February 11, 1946, ibid., 9:4225; see also idem before the Hart Inquiry, June 6, 1944, ibid., 26:469; idem before the NCI, August 31, 1944, ibid., 33:806–7.
42. Wohlstetter, *Pearl Harbor,* p. 219.
43. Testimony of Otis K. Sadtler before the joint committee, February 15, 1946, *Hearings,* 10:4629–30; idem before the APHB, October 6, 1944, ibid., 29: 2429–30; idem before the Clarke Inquiry, September 16, 1944, ibid., 34:67–68.
44. Exhibit 32, document 20, ibid., 14:1334; affidavit of Moses W. Pettigrew before the Clausen Investigation, February 12, 1945, ibid., 35:23–24.
45. Wohlstetter, *Pearl Harbor,* p. 64.
46. *Report of the Joint Committee,* p. 474; testimony of Rufus S. Bratton before the joint committee, February 14, 1946, *Hearings,* 9: 4540.
47. Affidavit of Harry L. Dawson and John E. Russel before the Clausen Investigation, April 16, 1945, ibid., 35:42. For further details about Wilkinson, see affidavit of Charles Willoughby before the Clausen Investigation, May 8, 1945, ibid., p. 86.
48. Testimony of Henry Clausen before the joint committee, February 12, 1946, ibid., 9:4336.
49. Thorpe to War Department, December 5, 1941, ibid., 18:3304.
50. Elliot R. Thorpe, *East Wind, Rain* (Boston: Gambit, 1969), pp. 51–55.
51. See reports from Gen. Douglas MacArthur, *Hearings,* 18:3307–10.
52. Ibid., p. 3306.
53. Ibid., pp. 3324–31.
54. Takeo Yoshikawa, "Top Secret Assignment," p. 38.
55. See Farago, *Broken Seal,* p. 328; *New York Times,* June 11, 1946.
56. See Rome to Tokyo #740, November 20, 1941, *Hearings,* 35: 670; Rio de Janeiro to Tokyo #482, November 30, 1941, ibid., p. 684; see also testimony of Laurence F. Safford before the

joint committee, February 1, 1946, ibid., 8:3581.

57. Tokyo to Washington #2444, December 1, 1941, ibid., 12: 209.

58. Testimony of Laurence F. Safford before the joint committee, February 1, 1946, ibid., 8:3584–85.

59. Tokyo to London #2494, December 7, 1941, ibid., 35:686.

60. Testimony of Owen Roberts before the joint committee, January 28, 1946, ibid., 7:3272; Proceedings of the Roberts Commission, ibid., 22:176, 192.

61. Testimony of Owen Roberts before the joint committee, January 28, 1946, ibid., 7:3276–78.

62. See documents 42, 43, and 44, Exhibit 37, ibid., 14:1408; testimony of Laurence F. Safford before the joint committee February 1, 1946, ibid., 8:3587–88.

63. Testimony of Otis K. Sadtler before the Clarke Inquiry, July 14, 1945, ibid., 34:87.

64. Testimony of Laurence F. Safford before the joint committee, February 4, 1946, ibid., 8:3685.

65. See memorandum by Sally T. Lightle, November 8, 1945, ibid., 18:3312–14.

66. Testimony of Alwin D. Kramer before the joint committee, February 8, 1946, ibid., 9:4060, 4063.

67. Wohlstetter, *Pearl Harbor*, p. 218.

68. See testimony of Harold Stark before the joint committee, January 5, 1946, *Hearings,* 5:2468; testimony of Henry Clausen before the joint committee, February 13, 1946, ibid., 9:4425–26.

69. Quoted in a memorandum by Safford to Commander Sonnett, May 14, 1945, from an earlier memorandum, ibid., 18:3349.

70. Testimony of Lester Schulz before the joint committee, February 15, 1946, ibid., 10:4662. The message being referred to may be found in Exhibit 1, ibid., 12:239–45.

71. Testimony of Laurence Safford before the joint committee, February 4, 1946, ibid., 8:3715, 3717.

72. Ibid., p. 3684.

73. Safford to C. C. Hiles, April 4, 1967, Hiles Papers, University of Wyoming Library, Laramie, Wyoming.

74. *Report of the Joint Committee,* p. 481.

75. "Minority Views," ibid., p. 32; Beard, *President Roosevelt,* p. 536.

Chapter 7

1. Lawrence Dennis to General Robert Wood, November 19, 1942, Wood Papers, Hoover Presidential Library, West Branch, Iowa.
2. Sherwood, *Roosevelt and Hopkins,* p. 827.
3. Harry S. Truman to Senator Harley Kilgore, September 14, 1945, Truman Papers, Office File, Truman Library, Independence, Mo.
4. William S. White, "Pearl Harbor Inquiry Revives Pre-War Debate: Echoes of Its Isolation-Intervention Arguments Are Heard Again," *New York Times,* December 2, 1945.
5. Norman Cousins, "Beyond Pearl Harbor," *Saturday Review of Literature,* December 8, 1945.
6. "The Story of Pearl Harbor," *New Republic,* December 10, 1945, pp. 782–83.
7. Allan Nevins, " 'A Challenge to Historic Truth,' " *New York Times Magazine,* December 16, 1945, pp. 8, 32–35.
8. John W. Owens, "Confusion Again Rules the GOP," *Baltimore Sun,* quoted in U.S. Congress, *Congressional Record,* December 21, 1945, p. A5755.
9. Henry L. Stimson to Thomas W. Lamont, January 3, 1946, Stimson Papers, Yale University Library, New Haven, Conn.
10. William Henry Chamberlin, "Shifting American Alignments," *Human Events,* May 22, 1946; idem, *Evolution of a Conservative,* pp. 181–93.
11. Quoted in Cole, *Charles A. Lindbergh,* p. 235; see also Lindbergh, *Wartime Journals,* p. xiii.
12. Felix Morley, "The Early Days of *Human Events,*" *Human Events,* April 27, 1974, pp. 394–99, reprinted in *Reason,* February 1978, pp. 32–36; Felix Morley to author, August 16, 1975.
13. Henry W. Berger, "A Conservative Critique of Containment: Senator Taft and the Early Cold War Program," in David Horowitz, ed., *Containment and Revolution* (Boston: Beacon, 1967), pp. 125–39; idem, "Senator Robert A. Taft Dissents From Military Escalation," in Thomas G. Paterson, ed., *Cold War Critics,* (Chicago: Quadrangle, 1971), pp. 167–204; Radosh, *Prophets,* pp. 119–95.
14. Radosh, *Prophets;* Joseph Stromberg, "The Cold War and the Transformation of the American Right: The Decline of Right-

Wing Liberalism," (Master's thesis: Florida Atlantic University, 1971); Justus D. Doenecke, "The 'Old' Isolationists and the Cold War, 1943–1954: An Ideology in Transition" (Unpublished manuscript at the Institute for Humane Studies, Menlo Park, Calif., 1975); Murray N. Rothbard, "Confessions of a Right-Wing Liberal," *Ramparts,* June 15, 1968; idem, "The Transformation of the American Right," *Continuum,* Summer 1964, pp. 220–31.

15. Beard in particular maintained that his criticism of interventionism began with the Philippine episode in 1899; see Charles A. Beard to George Morgenstern, April 11, 1948, and May 3, 1948, Morgenstern Papers, University of Wyoming Library, Laramie, Wyoming. The true nature of the old anti-imperialists' position has often been misinterpreted; the best analysis can be found in William Marina, "Opponents of Empire: An Interpretation of American Anti-Imperialism, 1898–1921" (Doctoral dissertation: University of Denver, 1968).

16. Samuel Eliot Morison, "Did Roosevelt Start the War? History Through a Beard," *Atlantic Monthly,* August 1948.

17. See, for example, Harry Elmer Barnes, *The Court Historians versus Revisionism* (n.p., n.d.).

18. Alfred A. Knopf to Richard N. Current, May 25, 1953; Roger W. Shugg to Richard N. Current, July 23, 1953; Richard N. Current to author, October 22, 1975; all in possession of author. On Beard, see Charles A. Beard to George Morgenstern, May 23 (1947?), Morgenstern Papers.

19. The text of Robert A. Theobald's *Final Secret of Pearl Harbor* (New York: Devin-Adair, 1954) appeared in *U.S. News and World Report,* April 2, 1954; the text of *Admiral Kimmel's Story* also appeared in *U.S. News and World Report,* December 10, 1954.

Bibliography

Manuscript Collections

Cambridge, Massachusetts. Harvard University. Joseph C. Grew Papers.

Eugene, Oregon. University of Oregon. John T. Flynn Papers.

Hyde Park, New York. Franklin D. Roosevelt Presidential Library. Franklin D. Roosevelt Papers.

Independence, Missouri. Harry S. Truman Presidential Library. Samuel I. Rosenman Papers.

————. Harry S. Truman Papers.

Laramie, Wyoming. University of Wyoming. Harry Elmer Barnes Papers.

————. Charles C. Hiles Papers.

————. Husband E. Kimmel Papers.

————. George Morgenstern Papers.

————. William L. Neumann Papers.

————. Laurence F. Safford Papers.

New Haven, Connecticut. Yale University. Henry L. Stimson Papers.

New York, New York. Columbia University Oral History Project. Interview with Adm. Thomas Hart.

————. Interview with Adm. Kent Hewitt.

————. Interview with Adm. Royal E. Ingersoll.

Princeton, New Jersey. Princeton University. James Forrestal Papers.

Stanford, California. Hoover Institution on War, Revolution and Peace. Robert A. Theobald Papers.

Washington, D.C. Library of Congress. Cordell Hull Papers.

West Branch, Iowa. Herbert C. Hoover Presidential Library. Bonner Fellers Papers.

———. Herbert C. Hoover Papers.

———. Verne Marshall Papers.

———. Westbrook Pegler Papers.

———. Charles C. Tansill Papers.

———. Walter Trohan Papers.

———. Robert Wood Papers.

Unpublished Works

Bartlett, Bruce R. "The Politics of Pearl Harbor, 1941–1946." Master's thesis, Georgetown University, 1976.

Doenecke, Justus. "The 'Old' Isolationists and the Cold War, 1943–1954: An Ideology in Transition." Unpublished manuscript at the Institute for Humane Studies, Menlo Park, California, 1975.

Frey, Richard C. "John T. Flynn and the United States in Crisis, 1928–1950." Doctoral dissertation, University of Oregon, 1969.

Marina, William. "Opponents of Empire: An Interpretation of American Anti-Imperialism, 1898–1921." Doctoral dissertation, University of Denver, 1968.

Stenehjem, Michele. "John Thomas Flynn and the New York Chapter of the America First Committee: Noninterventionism in the Northeast, 1940–41." Doctoral dissertation, State University of New York at Albany, 1975.

Stromberg, Joseph. "The Cold War and the Transformation of the American Right: The Decline of Right-Wing Liberalism." Master's thesis, Florida Atlantic University, 1971.

Government Documents

U.S. Congress, Joint Committee on the Investigation of the Pearl Harbor Attack. *Hearings Before the Joint Committee on the Investigation of the Pearl Harbor Attack,* 79th Cong., 1st sess., 39 pts. Washington, D.C.: U.S. Government Printing Office, 1946.

———. *Report of the Joint Committee on the Investigation of the Pearl Harbor Attack,* 79th Cong., 2d sess. Washington, D.C.: U.S. Government Printing Office, 1946.

U.S. Department of State. *Papers Relating to the Foreign Relations of the United States: Japan, 1931–1941,* 2 vols. Washington, D.C.: U.S. Government Printing Office, 1943.

————. *Peace and War: United States Foreign Policy, 1931–1941.* Washington, D.C.: U.S. Government Printing Office, 1943.

Books and Pamphlets

Adler, Selig. *The Isolationist Impulse.* New York: Abelard-Schuman, 1957.

Bailey, Thomas A. *The Man in the Street: The Impact of American Public Opinion on Foreign Policy.* New York: Macmillan, 1948.

Barkley, Alben W. *That Reminds Me.* Garden City, New York: Doubleday, 1954.

Barnes, Harry Elmer, ed. *Perpetual War for Perpetual Peace.* Caldwell, Idaho: The Caxton Printers, 1953.

Barnet, Richard. *Roots of War.* New York: Antheneum, 1972.

Beard, Charles A. *American Foreign Policy in the Making, 1932–1940.* New Haven, Conn.: Yale University Press, 1946.

————. *Giddy Minds and Foreign Quarrels.* New York: Macmillan, 1939.

————. *President Roosevelt and the Coming of the War, 1941.* New Haven, Conn.: Yale University Press, 1948.

Blum, John Morton. *From the Morgenthau Diaries: Years of Urgency, 1938–1941.* Boston: Houghton Mifflin, 1965.

Borchard, Edwin and Lage, William Potter. *Neutrality for the United States.* New Haven, Conn.: Yale University Press, 1937.

Borg, Dorothy and Okamoto, Shumpei, eds. *Pearl Harbor as History: Japanese-American Relations, 1931–1941.* New York: Columbia University Press, 1973.

Brownlow, Donald G. *The Accused: The Ordeal of Rear Admiral Husband Edward Kimmel, U.S.N.* New York: Vantage Press, 1968.

Butow, Robert J. C. *Tojo and the Coming of the War.* Princeton, N.J.: Princeton University Press, 1961.

Cantril, Hadley. *Public Opinion, 1935–1946.* Princeton, N.J.: Princeton University Press, 1951.

Chamberlin, William Henry. *America's Second Crusade.* Chicago: Regnery, 1950.

————. *The Evolution of a Conservative.* Chicago: Regnery, 1959.

Churchill, Winston S. *The End of the Beginning*. Boston: Little, Brown, 1943.

———. *The Grand Alliance*. Boston: Houghton Mifflin, 1951.

———. *Their Finest Hour*. Boston: Houghton Mifflin, 1949.

Clark, Ronald. *The Man Who Broke Purple*. Boston: Little, Brown, 1977.

Cole, Wayne S. *America First*. Madison, Wisconsin: University of Wisconsin Press, 1953.

———. *Charles A. Lindbergh and the Battle Against American Intervention in World War II*. New York: Harcourt Brace Jovanovich, 1974.

Compton, James V. *The Swastika and the Eagle*. Boston: Houghton Mifflin, 1967.

Current, Richard N. *Secretary Stimson: A Study in Statecraft*. New Brunswick, New Jersey: Rutgers University Press, 1954.

Davis, Forrest and Lindley, Ernest K. *How War Came*. New York: Simon and Schuster, 1942.

Divine, Robert A. *Foreign Policy and U.S. Presidential Elections*. New York: New Viewpoints, 1974.

———. *The Illusion of Neutrality*. Chicago: University of Chicago Press, 1962.

———. *Roosevelt and World War II*. Baltimore: Johns Hopkins Press, 1969.

Doenecke, Justus. *The Literature of Isolationism: A Guide to Non-Interventionist Scholarship, 1930–1972*. Colorado Springs, Colorado: Ralph Myles, 1972.

Dyer, George C. *On the Treadmill to Pearl Harbor: The Memoirs of Admiral James O. Richardson*. Washington, D.C.: U.S. Government Printing Office, 1973.

Farago, Ladislas. *The Broken Seal*. New York: Random House, 1967.

Feis, Herbert. *The Road to Pearl Harbor*. Princeton, N.J.: Princeton University Press, 1950.

Fish, Hamilton. *FDR: The Other Side of the Coin*. New York: Vantage Press, 1976.

Flynn, John T. *The Final Secret of Pearl Harbor*. New York: privately printed, 1945.

———. *The Truth About Pearl Harbor*. New York: privately printed, 1944.

Gardner, Lloyd C. *Economic Aspects of New Deal Diplomacy*. Boston: Beacon, 1971.

Gibson, Hugh, ed. *The Ciano Diaries, 1939–1943*. Garden City, New York: Doubleday, 1946.

179

Grew, Joseph C. *Ten Years in Japan.* New York: Simon and Schuster, 1944.

———. *Turbulent Era: A Diplomatic Record of Forty Years, 1904–1945.* Boston: Houghton Mifflin, 1952.

Griswold, A. Whitney. *The Far Eastern Policy of the United States.* New York: Harcourt, Brace and Company, 1938.

Hoehling, A. A. *The Week Before Pearl Harbor.* New York: Norton, 1963.

Horowtiz, David, ed. *Containment and Revolution.* Boston: Beacon, 1967.

Hull, Cordell. *The Memoirs of Cordell Hull,* 2 vols. New York: Macmillan, 1948.

Hyde, H. Montgomery. *Room 3603.* New York: Farrar, Straus, 1963.

Ickes, Harold L. *The Secret Diary of Harold L. Ickes: The Lowering Clouds, 1939–1941.* New York: Simon and Schuster, 1954.

Jonas, Manfred. *Isolationism in America, 1935–1941.* Ithaca, New York: Cornell University Press, 1966.

Kahn, David. *The Codebreakers.* New York: Macmillan, 1967.

Kase, Toshikazu. *Journey to the Missouri.* New Haven, Conn.: Yale University Press, 1950.

Kennan, George F. *American Diplomacy, 1900–1950.* Chicago: University of Chicago Press, 1951.

Kimball, Warren F. *The Most Unsordid Act: Lend-Lease, 1939–1941.* Baltimore: Johns Hopkins Press, 1969.

Kimmel, Husband E. *Admiral Kimmel's Story.* Chicago: Regnery, 1955.

Kirby, S. Winburn. *The War Against Japan: The Loss of Singapore.* London: Her Majesty's Stationery Office, 1957.

Kolko, Gabriel. *The Politics of War.* New York: Random House, 1968.

Krock, Arthur. *Memoirs.* New York: Funk and Wagnals, 1968.

Langer, William L. and Gleason, S. Everett. *The Challenge to Isolation.* New York: Harper and Brothers, 1952.

———. *The Undeclared War.* New York: Harper and Brothers, 1953.

Leighton, Isabel, ed. *The Aspirin Age, 1919–1941.* New York: Simon and Schuster, 1949.

Leopold, Richard. *The Growth of American Foreign Policy.* New York: Knopf, 1962.

Liggio, Leonard and Martin, James J., eds. *Watershed of Empire: Essays on New Deal Foreign Policy.* Colorado Springs, Colorado: Ralph Myles, 1976.

Lindbergh, Charles A. *The Wartime Journals of Charles A. Lindbergh.* New York: Harcourt Brace Jovanovich, 1970.

Melosi, Martin V. *The Shadow of Pearl Harbor: Political Controversy Over the Surprise Attack, 1941–1946.* College Station, Texas: Texas A & M University Press, 1977.

Millis, Walter, ed. *The Forrestal Diaries.* New York: Viking, 1951.

Morison, Samuel Eliot. *The Two-Ocean War.* Boston: Atlantic Monthly Press / Little, Brown, 1963.

Morgenstern, George. *Pearl Harbor: The Story of the Secret War.* New York: Devin-Adair, 1947.

Neumann, William L. *America Encounters Japan: From Perry to MacArthur.* Baltimore: Johns Hopkins Press, 1963.

————. *The Genesis of Pearl Harbor.* Philadelphia: The Pacifist Research Bureau, 1945.

Parkinson, Roger. *Blood, Toil, Tears and Sweat.* New York: David McKay, 1973.

Paterson, Thomas G., ed. *Cold War Critics.* Chicago: Quadrangle, 1971.

Pogue, Forrest C. *George C. Marshall: Ordeal and Hope, 1939–1942.* New York: Viking, 1966.

————. *George C. Marshall: Organizer of Victory, 1943–1945.* New York: Viking, 1973.

Radosh, Ronald. *Prophets on the Right.* New York: Simon and Schuster, 1975.

Russett, Bruce M. *No Clear and Present Danger: A Skeptical View of the U.S. Entry into World War II.* New York: Harper and Row, 1972.

Schroeder, Paul W. *The Axis Alliance and Japanese-American Relations, 1941.* Ithaca, New York: Cornell University Press, 1958.

Sherwood, Robert. *Roosevelt and Hopkins.* New York: Harper and Brothers, 1948.

Shigenori, Togo. *The Cause of Japan.* New York: Simon and Schuster, 1956.

Standley, William H. and Ageton, Arthur A. *Admiral Ambassador to Russia.* Chicago: Regnery, 1955.

Stenehjem, Michele. *An American First.* New Rochelle, New York: Arlington House, 1976.

Stevenson, William. *A Man Called Intrepid.* New York: Harcourt Brace Jovanovich, 1976.

Stimson, Henry L. and Bundy, McGeorge. *On Active Service in Peace and War.* New York: Harper and Brothers, 1948.

Theobald, Robert A. *The Final Secret of Pearl Harbor.* New York: Devin-Adair, 1954.

Thorpe, Elliot R. *East Wind, Rain.* Boston: Gambit, 1969.

Toland, John. *But Not in Shame: The Six Months After Pearl Harbor.* New York: Random House, 1961.

——. *The Rising Sun.* New York: Random House, 1970.

Tolley, Kemp. *Cruise of the Lanikai: Incitement to War.* Annapolis, Maryland: Naval Institute Press, 1973.

Wallin, Homer N. *Pearl Harbor: Why, How, Fleet Salvage and Final Appraisal.* Washington, D.C.: U.S. Government Printing Office, 1968.

Watson, Mark S. *Chief of Staff: Prewar Plans and Operations.* Washington, D.C.: U.S. Government Printing Office, 1950.

Welles, Sumner. *Seven Decisions That Shaped History.* New York: Harper and Brothers, 1951.

Wigmore, Lionel. *The Japanese Thrust.* Canberra, Australia, 1957.

Williams, William A. *The Tragedy of American Diplomacy.* New York: Delta, 1962.

Willoughby, Charles A. and Chamberlain, John. *MacArthur: 1941–1951.* New York: McGraw-Hill, 1954.

Wilson, Theodore. *The First Summit.* Boston: Houghton Mifflin, 1969.

Winterbotham, F. W. *The Ultra Secret.* New York: Harper and Row, 1974.

Wohlstetter, Roberta. *Pearl Harbor: Warning and Decision.* Stanford, California: Stanford University Press, 1962.

Woodward, Llewellyn. *British Foreign Policy in the Second World War,* 5 vols. London: Her Majesty's Stationery Office, 1970.

Yardley, Herbert O. *The American Black Chamber.* London: Faber and Faber, 1931.

Young, Roland. *Congressional Politics in the Second World War.* New York: Columbia University Press, 1956.

Articles

Adams, Frederick C. "The Road to Pearl Harbor: A Reexamination of American Far Eastern Policy, July 1937–December 1938." *Journal of American History* 58 (June 1971): 73–92.

Anderson, Irvine H. "The 1941 *De Facto* Embargo on Oil to Japan:

A Bureaucratic Reflex." *Pacific Historical Review* 44 (May 1975): 201–31.

Barnes, Harry Elmer. "The Final Story of Pearl Harbor." *Left and Right: A Journal of Libertarian Thought* 4 (1968).

Bartlett, Bruce R. "The Pearl Harbor Coverup." *Reason,* February 1976, pp. 24–27.

Beatty, Frank E. "Background of the Secret Report." *National Review,* 13 December 1966, pp. 1261–65.

Bolles, Blair. "Isolationists Use Pearl Harbor to Attack F.D.R. Policies." *Foreign Policy Bulletin,* November 30, 1945.

Burtness, Paul S. and Ober, Warren U. "Research Methodology: Problem of Pearl Harbor Intelligence Reports." *Military Affairs,* Fall 1961, 132–46.

———. "Secretary Stimson and the First Pearl Harbor Investigation." *Australian Journal of Politics and History* 14 (Spring 1968): 24–36.

Butow, Robert J. C. "Backdoor Diplomacy in the Pacific: The Proposal for a Konoye-Roosevelt Meeting, 1941." *Journal of American History* 59 (June 1972): 48–72.

———. "The Hull-Nomura Conversations: A Fundamental Misconception." *American Historical Review* 65 (July 1960): 822–36.

Chamberlain, John. "The Man Who Pushed Pearl Harbor." *Life,* April 1, 1946.

———. "Pearl Harbor." *Life,* September 24, 1945.

Chamberlin, William Henry. "Shifting American Alignments." *Human Events,* May 22, 1946.

Cole, Wayne S. "American Entry into World War II: A Historiographical Appraisal." *Mississippi Valley Historical Review* 43 (March 1957): 595–617.

Cousins, Norman. "Beyond Pearl Harbor." *Saturday Review of Literature,* December 8, 1945.

Current, Richard N. "How Stimson Meant to 'Maneuver' the Japanese." *Mississippi Valley Historical Review* 40 (June 1953): 67–74.

Dupuy, T. N. "Pearl Harbor: Who Blundered?" *American Heritage,* February 1962, pp. 65–81.

Esthus, Raymond A. "President Roosevelt's Commitment to Britain to Intervene in a Pacific War." *Mississippi Valley Historical Review* 50 (June 1963): 28–38.

Ferrell, Robert H. "Pearl Harbor and the Revisionists." *The Historian* 17 (Spring 1955): 215–33.

Greaves, Percy L. "FDR's Watergate: Pearl Harbor." *Reason*, February 1976, pp. 16–23.

———. "Pearl Harbor." *National Review*, December 13, 1966, pp. 1266–72.

Hiles, Charles C. "The Kita Message: Forever a Mystery?" *Chicago Tribune*, December 7, 1966.

———. "Marshall and Vietnam." *Rampart Journal*, Fall 1967, pp. 31–42.

———. "Roberta Wohlstetter's *Pearl Harbor: Warning and Decision.*" *Rampart Journal*, Winter 1966, pp. 82–95.

Hill, Norman. "Was There an Ultimatum Before Pearl Harbor?" *American Journal of International Law* 42 (1948): 355–67.

Hosoya, Chihiro. "Miscalculations in Deterrent Policy: Japanese-U.S. Relations, 1938–1941." *Journal of Peace Research*, 1968, pp. 97–115.

Kimball, Warren F. " 'Beggar My Neighbor': America and the British Interim Finance Crisis, 1940–1941." *Journal of Economic History* 29 (December 1969): 758–72.

———. "Churchill and Roosevelt: The Personal Equation." *Prologue: The Journal of the National Archives*, Fall 1974, pp. 169–82.

———. "Lend-Lease and the Open Door: The Temptation of British Opulence, 1937–1942." *Political Science Quarterly* 86 (June 1971): 232–59.

Miles, Sherman. "Pearl Harbor in Retrospect." *Atlantic Monthly*, July 1948, pp. 65–72.

Morison, Samuel Eliot. "Did Roosevelt Start the War? History Through a Beard." *Atlantic Monthly*, August 1948, pp. 91–97.

Morley, Felix. "The Early Days of *Human Events.*" *Human Events*, April 27, 1974, pp. 394–99.

Neumann, William L. "Franklin D. Roosevelt and Japan, 1913–1933." *Pacific Historical Review*, May 1953, pp. 143–53.

Nevins, Allan. " 'A Challenge to Historic Truth.' " *New York Times Magazine.* December 16, 1945, pp. 8, 32–35.

Richardson, Seth W. "Why Were We Caught Napping at Pearl Harbor?" *Saturday Evening Post*, May 24, 1947, pp. 20–21, 76.

Rothbard, Murray N. "Confessions of a Right-Wing Liberal." *Ramparts*, June 15, 1968, pp. 48–52.

———. "The Transformation of the American Right." *Continuum*, Summer 1968, pp. 220–31.

Tolley, Kemp. "The Strange Assignment of the USS *Lanikai.*" U.S. Naval Institute *Proceedings*, September 1962, pp. 70–83.

————. "The Strange Mission of the *Lanikai*." *American Heritage,* October 1973, pp. 57–95.

Truman, Harry S. "Our Armed Forces Must Be Unified." *Collier's,* August 26, 1944, pp. 16, 63–64.

Utley, Jonathan. "Upstairs, Downstairs at Foggy Bottom: Oil Exports and Japan, 1940–41." *Prologue: The Journal of the National Archives,* Spring 1976, pp. 17–28.

Villard, Oswald Garrison. "The Pearl Harbor Report." *Current History* 2 (March 1942): 11–13.

Yoshikawa, Takeo. "Top Secret Assignment." U.S. Naval Institute *Proceedings,* December 1960, pp. 27–39.

Index